T0360458

"The book, weaving together topical issues from intersections of identities, disaster resilience, healthcare, human resource management, approaches by public and non-profit organizations in crisis management, and the challenge of equity, provides evidence and interesting contemporary debates. The examples offered are timely, and illustrate clearly both how and why intersectionality is a critical component of effective, equitable, and fair crisis management. This text will be a must-read for both academics and practitioners in the fields of crisis/emergency management, diversity and inclusion, social equity!"

– **Mary E. Guy,** *PhD, Distinguished Professor, School of Public Affairs, University of Colorado, Denver*

"Resilience demands cohesive communities, interwoven social fabric, and democratic strengths. *Intersectionality and Crisis Management: A Path to Social Equity* provides a timely and important addition to growing interdisciplinary literature. This edited volume utilizes intersectionality to better inform crisis management in building resilient communities with specific emphasis on social equity and community vulnerabilities."

– **Naim Kapucu,** *PhD, Pegasus Professor, School of Public Administration & School of Politics, Security, and International Affairs, University of Central Florida*

"*Intersectionality and Crisis Management: A Path to Social Equity* addresses important social equity issues at a time where crisis management is becoming increasingly important in public, nonprofit, and health organizations. Readers will appreciate diverse perspectives from both established and emerging scholars."

– **Andy Crosby,** *PhD, Assistant Professor of Instruction, Master of Arts in Public Policy and Administration Program, Northwestern University*

"*Intersectionality and Crisis Management: A Path to Social Equity* is a timely book given unprecedented global crises such as the pandemic, economic recession, natural and environmental disasters, etc. The book provides thought-provoking discussions on how crises expose population groups to vulnerabilities and social equity challenges. A unique contribution of the book is the incorporation of an intersectional lens to expose social equity challenges because the impact of crises are felt at varying degrees by different people. The book, weaving together topical issues from intersections of identities, disaster resilience, healthcare, human resource management, approaches by public and non-profit organizations in crisis management, and the challenge of equity, provides evidence and interesting contemporary debates. Scholars and policy practitioners will find this book of interest in managing crises across social groups for building more resilient communities."

> – **Karen Johnston,** *PhD, Professor of Organisational Studies at the University of Portsmouth, and Associate Dean for Research and Innovation for the Faculty of Business and Law*

"*Intersectionality and Crisis Management: A Path to Social Equity* is an edited volume that utilizes intersectionality to better inform crisis management in building resilient communities with specific emphasis on social equity brings important insights into social equity issues at a time where crisis management is becoming increasingly important in public, nonprofit, and health organizations. Readers will appreciate diverse perspectives from both established and emerging scholars."

> – **Phin Xaypangna,** *Diversity, Equity & Inclusion Officer, County of Ventura, California*

"This volume offers a much-needed examination of issues of race, gender, sexual orientation, ethnicity, and socioeconomic factors and the ways in which these issues play out in crisis management. The various treatments presented by the contributing authors offer a compelling and insightful case for intersectionality in crisis management. The examples offered are timely, and illustrate clearly both how and why intersectionality is a critical component of effective, equitable, and fair crisis management. This text will be a must-read for both academics and practitioners in the fields of crisis/emergency management, diversity and inclusion, social equity, and intersectionality. Highly recommended!"

> – **John C. Morris,** *PhD, Professor Auburn University*

Intersectionality and Crisis Management

Intersectionality and Crisis Management: A Path to Social Equity aims to embed the social equity discourse into crisis management while exploring the potential of a new tool, the Integrative Crisis Management Model. Leaders and managers navigate a complex and networked environment of policy-making and action, frequently occurring in real time, under constant media exposure. The pervasive availability of this news on all platforms and devices produces a lingering anxiety about the inevitability of danger. Consequently, crisis affords a time-sensitive exploration of management practices and sheds a critical spotlight on deficiencies that may yield novel approaches to doing business.

As the book engages contributing authors who are foremost in their field, it also includes practitioners, students, and junior scholars in a creative new discourse about equity. Bringing these diverse voices together in one volume presents a unique opportunity to generate new insights. Intersectionality provides a framework for understanding how categorizations of people drive social constructs of discrimination and oppression. Each chapter covers a different subject – exploring intersectionality in healthcare, nonprofit management, and human resources – and is accompanied by discussion questions. The book provides something for the classroom, for practitioners, and for scholars who want to include more intersectional thinking into their work.

Hillary J. Knepper is a professor in the Department of Public Administration at Pace University, USA.

Michelle D. Evans is an assistant professor in the Department of Political Science and Public Service at the University of Tennessee at Chattanooga, USA.

Tiffany J. Henley is an assistant professor in the Department of Public Administration at Pace University, USA.

Routledge Focus on Issues in Global Talent Management
Series Editor: Ibraiz Tarique
Pace University, USA

Talent Management in Small and Medium Enterprises
Context, Practices and Outcomes
Aleksy Poctowski, Urban Pauli and Alicja Miś

Talent Management in Latin America
Pressing Issues and Best Practices
Edited by Jordi Trullen and Jaime Bonache

Intersectionality and Crisis Management
A Path to Social Equity
Edited by Hillary J. Knepper, Michelle D. Evans and Tiffany J. Henley

For more information about this series, please visit: www.routledge.com/ Routledge-Focus-on-Issues-in-Global-Talent-Management/book-series/ RFIGTM

Intersectionality and Crisis Management
A Path to Social Equity

Edited by Hillary J. Knepper, Michelle D. Evans and Tiffany J. Henley

NEW YORK AND LONDON

First published 2023
by Routledge
605 Third Avenue, New York, NY 10158

and by Routledge
4 Park Square, Milton Park, Abingdon, Oxon, OX14 4RN

Routledge is an imprint of the Taylor & Francis Group, an informa business

Library of Congress Cataloging-in-Publication Data
A catalog record for this book has been requested

ISBN: 978-1-032-02684-8 (hbk)
ISBN: 978-1-032-02685-5 (pbk)
ISBN: 978-1-003-18462-1 (ebk)

DOI: 10.4324/9781003184621

Typeset in Times New Roman
by Apex CoVantage, LLC

We dedicate our book to all of the folks whose daily lives place them at the forefront of crisis management and the rest of us, whose lives depend upon them.

Hillary J. Knepper: I dedicate this book to my wonderful colleagues who joined me on this adventure – from our chapter authors to Michelle and Tiffany who made our vision a reality. I also dedicate this to my family for their patience during this process, with a special dedication to my amazing husband David Klobus, who always has my back and who always comes through in the clutch.

Michelle D. Evans: I dedicate this book to my co-editors and all the amazing scholars and practitioners who participated in this project. And a special thank you to Hillary for asking me to be a part of the project and to Ellie and Hamilton for their support and stress relief.

Tiffany J. Henley: I dedicate this book to my family and friends for their ongoing support and assistance. I also want to acknowledge the academic trailblazers who have come before me for their efforts and for theorizing and operationalizing the constructs of intersectionality and crisis management.

Contents

Preface

This book has been an incredible learning experience and labor [of love] that started as an idea by Hillary J. Knepper back in 2020. As editors, we had a vision about where this book would take us and we knew who we hoped to work with on this project. We were beyond honored that our esteemed colleagues agreed to join us. As you will notice, the authors represented in this book are considered preeminent in their discipline. Bringing them together in one volume presents a unique opportunity to generate new insights about a fairly novel concept in management. This diversity of thought and experience led to the development of wonderful scholarship and new ways of thinking about our material. Through the challenges of these last two years, our contributing authors' contributions steadfastly helped us achieve our vision.

We have built our scholarship on an innovative tradition of women who have long been raising their voices – about abolition, voting rights, reproductive freedom, employment, and other issues of inequity. Perhaps one of the most recognized early feminist voices, Mary Wollenstonecraft, upended traditional scholarship in the 18th century with her "A Vindication of the Rights of Woman," about the social and economic injustices women then faced. Yet, the discipline of feminist theory really didn't find itself in the mainstream for another 150 years, where it finally rose to prominence during the 1960s and 1970s. This feminist perspective was considered a radical and disruptive new approach to scholarship and thinking about society. Yet it took another generation for gender-focused scholarship to gain traction in the public administration field, which didn't experience a significant expansion until the 1990s. This time, the discourse was led by heavy-hitter women scholars such as Mary Guy, Rita Mae Kelly, Norma Riccucci, Pat Shields, and Camilla Stivers, and in the 2000s by women such as Susan Gooden, Rosemary O'Leary, Sally Selden, and Jessica Sowa. In recent years, this scholarship began incorporating a broader view, recognizing the importance of overlapping demographic influences and impacts based on intersectionalities such as race, sexual orientation, and socioeconomics. New scholars began emerging in this new research area, led by Maria D'Agostino, Meghna Sabharwal, Brandi Blessett, Tia Sheree Gaynor, Sean McCandless, and countless others. This book, in many ways, stands on the shoulders of these amazing scholars, as well as groups such as Academic Women in Public Administration and the American Society for Public Administration's Section for Women in Public Administration.

If you will indulge us for a moment, we would like to explain the construction of this book as both a work of scholarship and a representation of the subject. The chapters in this book have intentionally been constructed to be intersectional in nature, meaning intersectional subject matter as well as intersectional in terms of authors and ideas. The book incorporates individuals representing a diverse range of race, ethnicities, gender identities, expertise, methodological approaches, and backgrounds. It also includes scholars ranging from doctoral students and early career scholars to established senior scholars. The book includes academics, medical professionals, nonprofit practitioners, and public sector personnel. The chapters represent individuals with research specialties in gender and race, healthcare, crisis management, leadership/management, social equity, ethics, pedagogy, human resources, and nonprofit administration. The structure of the book was designed to be shorter in hopes that it would translate into a quicker turnaround time, thus increasing the chances of the book and book chapters focusing on more time-sensitive subjects. Research has also shown that books assigned as reading in graduate education are disproportionately authored by men, while book chapters and journal articles assigned in classes are far more likely to have women authors. Therefore, our hope is that the structure (and ideally the more affordable price) of the book will increase the possibility of highlighting more intersectional representation within authorship and course readings.

We have a quick clarification for all you APA experts. We have intentionally chosen to use APA 6th edition for this book because of the in-text citation style (i.e. authors 2–5 are listed in the first in-text citation). In addition, we have modified the APA to include the full first name for authors instead of initials in the references. We gladly will sacrifice a few extra words here and there to increase the visibility and recognition for the wealth of amazing, diverse scholars within this subject matter.

During the editing process, the three of us have gained countless new insights into how to approach our own scholarship, how to work with others, and how to expand our networks of people, ideas, and methodologies. It is our hope that this project has served as a mentoring tool for those involved, providing one more element to help overcome barriers that are so often expanded by overlapping, intersectional demographics impacting career advancement for individuals. Finally, we hope this book provides new opportunities for classroom, scholarly, and workplace intersectional discourse both in crisis management and beyond. We'd love to hear how you use this book, so please let us know.

Hillary J. Knepper
Michelle D. Evans
Tiffany J. Henley

Acknowledgments

We would like to acknowledge all the amazing intersectional scholars who have influenced us as individuals in our own career paths, and especially those who contributed to, assisted with, and inspired this book. We are grateful to the anonymous reviewers, to the eagle-eyed proof-readers, to the research help from graduate assistants, university personnel, and to all those forgiving friends and family who offered patience, support, and assistance through this long project. And, of course, we are grateful to the wonderful contributing authors, and ask them to forward our thanks to all the countless individuals who helped them in their scholarship.

We would like to thank all the folks at Routledge, especially Jessica Rech, our dedicated editorial assistant, for her patience and guidance throughout this project. Last, but certainly not least, we extend our deep appreciation to Dr. Ibraiz Tarique, editor of the Focus Series on Global Talent Management at Routledge, for his encouragement in producing this book on crisis management and intersectionality.

Some special shout-outs for their above and beyond contributions are given to: Sebawit G. Bishu, Allison Bruce, Nicole M. Elias, Natalie Haber, Jose Luis Irizarry, David J. Klobus, Zoë A. Klobus, Claire Connolly Knox, Monette Moradi, Patricia M. Shields, Derek Slagle, Colton Strawser, and countless members of Academic Women in Public Administration and Section for Women in Public Administration.

About the Editors and Contributing Authors

Tony Carrizales, PhD, MPA is an associate professor of public administration at Marist College and chair of the Department of Public and Nonprofit Administration. His research interests include diversity in the public sector and e-government. His research has been published in *Public Performance and Management Review, Public Administration Quarterly, and State and Local Government Review*. Dr. Carrizales received his MPA from Cornell University and PhD in public administration from Rutgers University – Newark.

Ravin Cline is a third year PhD student in the Public and Nonprofit Management Program within the School of Economic, Political, and Policy Sciences at the University of Texas at Dallas. Her research interests span topics within the nonprofit sector. She is also interested in the use of co-production among the private, public, and nonprofit sectors to address social issues related to diversity, equity, and inclusion (DEI). She is currently the founder and executive director of Embracing Diversity, a 501(c)(3) founded to serve the immigrant community.

Fatih Demiroz, PhD is an associate professor at Sam Houston State University. He received his PhD in public affairs from the University of Central Florida. His research interests concentrate on social and organizational networks, disaster and crisis management, resilience, and complex systems. His recent publications include the *Journal of Homeland Security and Emergency Management*, and the *Journal of Emergency Management, and Local Government Studies*.

Schnequa Nicole Diggs, PhD, MPA is an assistant professor of public administration at North Carolina Central University. Her research interests include social, racial, and gender equity; intersectionality; and diversity, equity, and inclusion (DEI) in public administration. She has published in *Public Performance and Management Review, Administrative Theory* and *Praxis*, the *Journal of Affective Disorders Report, Teaching Public Administration*, and the *Journal of Public Health Finance*. She is an active member of ASPA currently serving on the COMPA and DSJ Board of Directors. She also serves on the Affordable Housing Implementation Committee for the City of Durham, NC.

Michelle D. Evans, PhD, MPA is an assistant professor at the University of Tennessee at Chattanooga specializing in nonprofit management and public administration. Her research focuses on gender equity, inclusive pedagogy, ethics, and nonprofit management. Her recent work has appeared in *Voluntas, Public Integrity, Review of Public Personnel Administration, Human Resource Management Review*, and *Teaching Public Administration*. She is a board member for the Friends of Cherokee National Forest nonprofit and serves on the editorial boards of the *Journal of Public Affairs Education* and the *Journal of Health and Human Services Administration*. She is a former chair of the ASPA Section for Women in Public Administration and recipient of the 2019 Marcia P. Crowley Award for service to SWPA. Prior to academia, she spent more than 20 years as a nonprofit practitioner, working primarily with Special Olympics.

Tiffany J. Henley, PhD is an assistant professor in the Department of Public Administration at Pace University specializing in public administration and healthcare administration. Her research focuses on identifying and evaluating policy initiatives and options, highlighting health and social inequities, and informing practitioners and policymakers to address equity issues in health and society. She has published in *Informatics for Health and Social Care, Journal of the National Black Association for Speech-Language and Hearing, Journal of Public Affairs Education*, and *Journal of Health Economics, Policy and Law*. She is the elected chair for the Section on Health and Human Services Administration which is affiliated with the American Society for Public Administration (ASPA). She is an editorial board member with the *Journal of Health and Human Services Administration*. She is also an active member of ASPA and member of American College of Healthcare Executives (ACHE).

Thanh Thi Hoang is a PhD candidate in the Public and Nonprofit Management Program, School of Economic, Political & Policy Sciences at the University of Texas at Dallas. Her research interests encompass both public and nonprofit management. In nonprofit management, she focuses on communication, resource mobilization, and community engagement. In public management, she is interested in human resources, diversity, and inclusion.

Hillary J. Knepper, PhD, MPA is the associate provost for student success and a full professor in the Department of Public Administration at Pace University. Prior to the Academy, she was an administrator in nonprofit and public sector organizations and brings this strong practitioner perspective to her research on gender equity and healthcare – with particular emphasis on marginalized and vulnerable populations. Her recent work can be found in *Public Administration Review, Teaching Public Administration, Journal of Public Affairs Education, Public Integrity*, and *Public Administration Quarterly*. She serves as the editor-in-chief of the *Journal of Health and Human Services Administration* and is the current co-president of Academic Women in Public Administration. Her recent media interviews include *Scripps National News* and a national podcast for *Public Integrity*. She was recognized by the American Society for Public Administration as one of 16 women in public administration and was featured in their *Profiles of Excellence*.

Rosa Castillo Krewson, PhD is an adjunct instructor in the Washington Semester Program at American University and is a graduate of the Center of Public Administration and Policy (CPAP) at Virginia Tech. Dr. Krewson's research centers on social equity in American politics and public policy. She is a 2017 Founders Fellow of the American Society for Public Administration (ASPA), 2018 Equity & Inclusion Fellow of the Association for Public Policy Analysis and Management (APPAM), and she received the 2019 Founders of CPAP Scholarship award. The Public Administration Theory Network selected her article for the Best Article of 2021 award.

Sean A. McCandless, PhD works at the University of Illinois Springfield's School of Public Management & Policy. He holds positions as assistant professor and as associate director of the Doctorate in Public Administration Program. His research centers on how governments can become fairer for all in terms of access, outcomes, processes, and quality of public services. With Dr. Mary E. Guy, he is co-editor of the book *Achieving Social Equity: From Problems to Solutions* (Melvin & Leigh), and has co-edited several scholarly journal volumes on social equity.

Nora Montalvo-Liendo, PhD is an associate professor at the School of Nursing-Texas A&M Health Science Center. As a bilingual, bicultural nurse in the Rio Grande Valley, Texas, she has established a long history of collaborations with several nonprofit community agencies, private medical practice clinics, and community health clinics to solve critical social problems. Dr. Montalvo-Liendo has successfully conducted qualitative and quantitative research on domestic violence. Her research focuses on developing, testing, and evaluating the efficacy of interventions to empower Hispanic survivors of abuse and to address the future well-being of Hispanic children with a history of adverse childhood experiences.

Meghna Sabharwal, PhD is a professor and program head in the public and nonprofit management program at the University of Texas at Dallas. Her research is focused on public human resources management, specifically diversity, equity, and inclusion. She is widely published in leading public administration journals and has received several best paper awards. She serves on several editorial boards and is the associate editor of the *Review of Public Personnel Administration* and *Public Integrity*.

Michelle Silverio, DPH is a director at Mount Sinai Department of Urology. She has previously managed multi-disciplinary school-based, urgent care, and Article 28 health centers. Dr. Silverio received her MPH from Yale University School of Public Health and DrPH in public health from CUNY Graduate School of Public Health and Health Policy. Her research on cultural competency has been published in *Public Administration Quarterly*.

Crystal Whetstone, PhD is an assistant professor at Bilkent University, in their Department of International Relations. Her research on gender and international and comparative politics focuses on the role political motherhood plays in Global South women's peace movements. Her recent scholarship has been published in *Women's Studies International Forum, Journal of the Motherhood Initiative*, and *Romanian Review of Political Sciences and International Relations*.

Illustrations and Tables

Figures

Tables

1 Considering Intersectionality and Its Implications for Crisis Management

Hillary J. Knepper, Michelle D. Evans, and Tiffany J. Henley

Introduction

We are living in an unprecedented time of crisis. It permeates our news, our social media, our own lives, and we live in a continuously heightened state of alert. Leaders and managers navigate a complex and networked environment of policy-making and action, frequently occurring in real time, under constant media exposure. The pervasive availability of this news from around the world, on virtually every platform and device, produces a lingering anxiety about the inevitability of danger. It isn't just the flooding in your state you have to worry about, now it's flooding far away on the other side of the world. A contaminated food or medical product doesn't just lead to a localized recall, it causes massive supply chain disruptions. Economic recession doesn't just affect your job, it is global, affecting millions of individuals. This perpetual state of emergency is broad in scope and it is unavoidable; whether the situation is widespread – war, natural disaster, recession – or personal – a house fire, the loss of a job, mental health challenges. Consequently, concerns over how public planning directs resources and distributes risk mitigation are now viewed in a global spotlight.

From water management to energy consumption, every decision creates downslope impact. Droughts, like those experienced in the American Southwest, evidence downslope impact. Tribal lands have long foreshadowed the larger scale drought, having faced perpetual water shortages. In 2022, multiple states are planning water utilization priorities to contend with the Colorado River volume loss. Some, like energy-planning, create both local and global challenges that result in competing resource demands. In turn, public policymaking and planning must decide which demands are met with public and private resources. How do we decide who gets the limited water resources in the American Southwest? Do we use our public resources to bolster another country's healthcare system during early-stage

DOI: 10.4324/9781003184621-1

health emergencies, before their arrival in our own country? Do we incentivize private business to build in protections against recessionary periods to avoid job loss at home? The choices are endless. Yet, these choices are made every day, by management decision-makers all over the world and in our own communities. The question is, what determinants are used to understand a fuller picture of the people adversely affected by these decisions in order to determine greater or lesser impact?

We suggest this new generational and pervasive exposure to news and information provides a turning point to reflect on the interconnected and often inequitable outcomes of leadership decisions. This live exposure means public management decisions can be assessed differently under the pressure of public scrutiny. This scrutiny demands answers about who is valued and who is not based upon how they are buffered from danger or calamity. This global spotlight exposes vulnerabilities and social equity challenges on a scale unseen before this generation. This constant exposure to catastrophe and injustice of course has the potential to desensitize us. But we argue instead that it can also have the opposite effect – shining a light on societal structural and moral underpinnings that weaken social systems and inequitably distribute risk and protection. It is for this reason that we turn the spotlight on crisis management.

At the same time, information availability is extending to changes in social norms. We're currently experiencing a growing awareness that people are defined not just by single attributes (gender or race or sexual orientation or socioeconomic strata or ethnicity, etc.) but by constructs of multiple *intersectional* attributes (gender and race and (dis)ability for example). These attributes more accurately reflect who we are and what we need based upon these human experiences (type of employment, caregiving responsibilities, (dis)ability, geography, nationality, religion, language, etc.). We've come to realize these ever-evolving constructs influence how public policies are made and implemented. In the context of this book, these constructs determine how we perceive potential problems and influence the degree to which we prepare for, manage, and recover from crisis, both as a society and as individuals. Because of the visibility of these policy outcomes, the lack of equity across these intersectional constructs is exposed. The unequal impact of the COVID-19 pandemic response on working women with children is one example of this, and it is discussed more thoroughly in subsequent chapters in this book.

This constant exposure to crisis and the emerging understanding of the impact of intersectionality led us to write this book. It is our intention to provide new insights, spur debate, and to recommend opportunities for improving equity in the context of this particularly complex public policy area. We acknowledge that change can be difficult and that transformation is ultimately a disruptive act. To this end, we adopt Blessett's (2020) assertion that there is "the potential of intersectionality to deconstruct and disarm the systems of domination" (p. 4) for the purpose of upending crisis management. Therefore, we urge readers to proceed through the subsequent chapters in this book with a critical eye toward disrupting the status quo to create more equitable practices.

To begin this transformative perspective, we reconceptualize crisis so it is contextualized differently. Understanding the impact of intersectionality affords us a time-sensitive exploration of management practices that often reveal catastrophic inequities. It is our hope that by applying an intersectional framework, we can improve resiliency outcomes. As a result of better-informed management decisions, we can ameliorate social inequities, leading to more comprehensive and inclusive preparations for, and recovery from, crisis. By considering the intersectional framework through which to structure crisis management, we demonstrate how contemporary crisis management can benefit through this timely understanding of intersectionality.

We begin our definition of intersectionality as "the crossing, juxtaposition, or meeting point, of two or more social categories and axes, or systems of power, dominance, or oppression" (Atewologun, 2018, p. 2). Over time, this understanding may yield novel approaches to crisis recovery or even methods of prevention. Indeed, Branicki (2020) argues for a transformational, feminist approach to crisis management, that moves beyond the traditional, rational, gendered, and racially hegemonic approach to crisis. She argues that applying Gilligan's (1993) ethics of care approach is more appropriate in that it is relationship oriented, building on the concept of leaving no one behind. Gilligan's work is notable for shifting the emphasis outside of male-dominated assumptions and perspectives and instead situates decision-making on helping and caring within relationship networks rather than centered in impartiality or neutrality. This is a basic tenet of understanding intersectionality.

Intersectionality provides a framework for understanding how categorizations of people drive social constructs of discrimination and oppression (Diggs, 2022). This results in bias and oppression, resulting in a loss of social and intellectual capital and opportunity that is recursive – creating an endless cycle of unbroken inequity and systemic privation. However, it can be challenging to overcome these deeply rooted categorizations of people and their associated social constructs. How clearly are we able to understand and respect differing cultural norms? Why does this matter? It matters a great deal for crisis managers and policy-makers. Indeed, Haupt and Connolly Knox (2018) identify that cultural competence has not been fully integrated into the emergency manager's toolkit, consequently, their ability to understand and best serve "socially vulnerable" populations is limited.

Clearly, cultural competence proficiency has been slow moving as it was traditionally promoted as a management concept, yet, it is still largely missing from public and private management decision-making. Cultural competence emerged to lead organizations in their work to incorporate the understanding of "cultural" difference in populations and to be proactive in creating policies that acknowledge and address these differences while also recruiting and training their workforce to understand the needs of a diverse citizenry (Borrego & Johnson III, 2017; Carrizales, Zahradnik, & Silverio, 2016). This can be particularly challenging as overlapping inter-sectionalities are often related to communication differences and trust issues linked to historical discrimination and oppression (Haupt, 2020; Wright & Merritt, 2020). While cultural competency has been a key initiative in the public sector and human resource management in recent years, the term itself implies an emphasis on social/cultural characteristics, such as race and gender. We recognize that viewing crisis through this framing also depends upon a foundation of cultural competence and therefore assert that it is time to re-imagine what is meant by cultural competence in light of crisis management and intersectionality.

Understanding how intersectionality affects management operations affords unique interdisciplinary theory building with implications for practice. Accordingly, we embed intersectionality into the academic and practitioner crisis management discourse. Cultural norms and civic action have the capacity to affect decision-making within the complex environment of crisis (Knox, Goodman, Entress, & Tyler, 2022). These norms and actions contribute to an intersectional lens, providing a clearer path to better preparedness and recovery. Ultimately, this improved resilience and recovery model will yield a more inclusive and equitable crisis response.

Foundations and Definitions

Crisis, in its various iterations, is one thing that all sectors, public, for-profit, and nonprofit, share in the understanding that it is not "if" but rather "when." The word "crisis" brings to mind different understandings and narratives. Basic definitions of crisis often focus on situations that require large-scale, urgent, or critical responses, situations that pose threats to lives, values, or structures (both physical and systemic), or situations that may have serious emotional impacts (Bundy, Pfarrer, Short, & Coombs, 2017; Christensen & Lægreid, 2020; Moon, Sasangohar, Son, & Peres, 2020). Others view this definition as too limited on decision-making elements and often overlooking or diminishing trauma as an ongoing element with disparate impacts (Mitroff & Alpaslan, 2020). Still others focus on the social construction of crisis in terms of the aftermath (Hutter & Lloyd-Bostock,

2013), with events "radically redefining" circumstances (Gilpin & Murphy, 2008, p. 4), with long-term implications on policies, practices, and/or reputations or career prospects for individuals or organizations (Bundy et al., 2017; Gilpin & Murphy, 2008).

Even the more simplified definition focusing on significant and/or unexpected situations outside the normal, day-to-day environment brings to mind different interpretations. These may include natural disasters such as hurricanes, floods, tornadoes, etc. that require emergency crisis management. These crises may be localized in a narrow geographic region (i.e. tornado), span significant areas on a national scale, or be multi-national or global (i.e. the 2004 tsunami that impacted multiple nations bordering the Indian Ocean or the recent COVID-19 pandemic). Other interpretations of "crisis" may be related to either a broader societal impact, such as an ecosystem, or more narrowed to small groups or individuals (see Ch 2, Whetstone & Demiroz, 2023). For instance, crisis in economics could mean the 2008 financial crisis or it could mean groups of employees or individual employees getting laid off. Similarly, health crisis could mean the aforementioned COVID-19 pandemic (see Ch 3, Silverio, Montalvo-Liendo, & Carrizales, 2023) or HIV/AIDS, policy changes regarding reproductive rights or access, or it could be the diagnosis of cancer, heart disease, etc. that significantly impacts an individual or families' well-being.

Crisis is often linked to the necessity of intersectoral assistance, spanning government, nonprofit, and for-profit sector partnerships (see Ch 5, Diggs, Castillo Krewson, & McCandless, 2023). More recently we have seen new interpretations of crisis emanating from shifts in social norms in areas such as sexual harassment (#MeToo) (Knepper, Scutelnicu, & Tekula, 2020) that have significantly impacted individuals, companies, and overall management practices. Crisis may also result in dramatic shifts in human resource management practices, such as the need for work-from-home due to the global pandemic (see Ch 4, Hoang, Cline, & Sabharwal, 2023). All of these situations are contributing to what can be considered the "*new normal*" for society and for management, with particular emphasis in this book on crisis management. We have adapted a definition of "*new normal*" from Tomsett (2020) to explain the context for its use throughout this book. We use his phrase to characterize trends that emerged during the COVID-19 pandemic that have affected our society in terms of workplace behaviors and tools, our changing expectations of the workplace, our responses to the crisis of the pandemic, and how we use technology for work.

Understanding intersectionality is more complex. Atewologun (2018) recently defined it on the most basic level as the intersection of two or more points. At the same time the definition highlights both the importance or urgency of the subject as well as providing glimpses into the depth of challenges by focusing on implications for power and oppression. These components highlight the general consensus on how the concept is often tackled in the literature, with one key approach focusing on the intersection of demographics and the evolution of our understanding of concepts such as gender or race.

Perhaps the most notable scholar on the subject of intersectionality, Kimberlé Crenshaw (1989, 1991, 2020) highlights society's tendency to focus on demographic categories as exclusive and defined, without the consideration of how categories of "difference" are often interrelated, overlapping, and therefore infinitely more complicated, with marginalization burdens and impacts building upon each other. When the term intersectionality first emerged, it was often framed and focused on the intersection of race and gender – but today the term is generally expanded to encompass a much broader range of intersecting and overlapping "difference" in many areas, building to include sexuality and gender identity, (dis)ability, class, etc. within theoretical applications involving hegemonic power and privilege and marginalized burdens and impacts (Breslin, Pandey, & Riccucci, 2017; Diggs, 2022; Jashinsky, King, Kwiat, Henry, & Lockett-Glover, 2021; Nash, 2008). Silberstein, Tramontano, and Nayak (2020) build upon the "intersections of . . . vectors of diversity" and expand the focus to include the challenge of navigating the social construction of identities with differing interpretations and ongoing evolution of societal understanding of these concepts that often include value judgments, privileges, and burdens (pp. 4-5).

The battles for intersectional equity are frequently framed as focused on external and existing power dynamics, such as the feminist movement battling against patriarchal practices limiting workplace access, advancement opportunities, and equal pay (Hamidullah & Riccucci, 2017). At the same time, intersectional power dynamics can be internal, such as the marginalization of Black or lesbian women in the early women's rights movement (Diggs, 2022; Pomerleau, 2010). These dynamics have been referred to as "political intersectionality" and "intersectional solidarity," combining elements of social construction with both the challenges and necessity of solidarity to achieve social change (Crowder & Smith, 2020).

Others focus their research on concepts of identity, power, and inequality through the lens of intersectionality, or as a variable for research into other concepts (Fay, Hicklin Fryar, Meier, & Wilkins, 2021), sometimes focusing on difference through "categories . . . processes . . . [or] systems of domination" (Dhamoon, 2011, p. 233). Patricia Hill Collins (2019) calls intersectionality both a critical methodology for research as well as a form of advocacy or action for social problems and inequity. This book focuses largely on the relevance of intersectionality as an analytical tool to better guide more inclusive and comprehensive crisis planning and to understand practices that have contributed to unequal treatment of groups that have been left behind and underserved due to their intersectional attributes.

Challenges of Intersectionality as a Lens

Despite the increased attention to intersectionality as a concept, and the increased recognition of the implications of intersectionality on policy design, management, and decision-making, intersectionality creates new battlegrounds for debate and understanding and uncovers inequitable impacts (many of which will be discussed in the following chapters). Perhaps the most basic of these considerations is that single attributes by themselves do not provide sufficient insight into understanding individuals or groups. Single attributes, such as gender or race or ethnicity or socioeconomic strata, alone are inadequate to understanding individuals and groups to sufficiently buffer them from crisis. Further, social, cultural, or other categories of difference (e.g. household conditions, caregiving, (dis)ability paired with a service animal, religion) also are not monolithic groups. Rather, it is the interactions of these varying intersectional attributes that provide clearer insight into individuals, groups, and communities, essential to effective crisis management. Within each group there may be countless subsets, each of which may overlap with other intersectionalities. For instance, race is one possible grouping, comprised of numerous subsets that have evolved over time. In the past, the U.S. Census Bureau has categorized race into five categories, White, Black/African American, Asian, Indigenous (American Indian/Alaska Native), and Native Hawaiian/Other Pacific Islander (U.S. Census Bureau, 2022). Yet, each of these categories represent numerous subgroupings, some examples of which are incorporated into Figure 1.1. Similarly, terminology changes. We see this evidenced in how "gender" is understood, moving from a traditional binary perspective into an expanded and evolving non-binary perspective (Klobus, Evans, & Knepper, 2022). But embracing a true intersectional frame for understanding individuals and groups means we must add in additional attributes that include things like religion, political affiliation, (dis)ability, caregiving responsibilities among countless others, and leads to crucial differences in understanding how circumstances and beliefs can mean a difference between inclusive crisis management practices and potentially dangerous neglectful practices. The data as illustrated in Figure 1.1 are by no means exhaustive of all possible intersectional attributes, but instead, the figure offers a visual aid to illustrate potential examples of these possibilities. There are unlimited definitions in how people and communities identify themselves. Effective crisis management depends upon not only recognizing these intersectional attributes, but

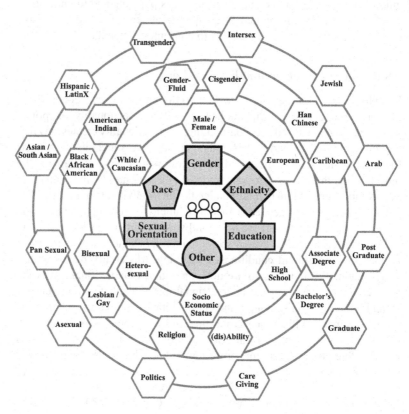

Figure 1.1 Expanding and Overlapping Intersectional Classifications

on identifying which are most important to reflect on and account for during crisis.

But even using these categories, we can take one group and break it down into countless others. For instance, "Asian" may mean an individual who resides in a host of different nations (e.g. Japan, China, Vietnam, etc.) while "South Asian" is used to differentiate still more categories (e.g. Bangladesh, Bhutan, India, Pakistan, Nepal, Sri Lanka), or it may mean someone living in the US who traces some or all of their heritage back to one of these nations. The U.S. Census has attempted to address some of the changing dynamics in regard to race/ethnicity and intersectionality, by adjusting their census forms to accommodate multiple responses for each individual (Marks & Rios-Vargas, 2021), thereby accommodating the increasing intersectional multiculturalism in society, as well as providing more flexibility in how people self-identify. But even these smaller classifications *are not* monolithic classifications, whereby individuals within are evermore in agreement on . . . anything. It is inevitable that fully understanding any group that consists of two or more members who share a major attribute (e.g. gender, race) will be complex due to their other intersectional attributes (e.g. socioeconomics, religion, caregiving responsibilities). For instance, two siblings could be raised in the same family, with the same parents, same race, gender, and economic background, both completing their public education at the same schools and both completing college degrees. Despite the seemingly similar demographics, these two siblings are completely different based upon other intersectional differences such as different interpretations of gender identity, introverted vs extroverted, theater buff vs sports fan, politics, religious practice (or lack of), living situation, caregiving responsibilities, etc. Even a mild difference in SAT scores could influence which college they attended, which impacts their future employment opportunities leading to different starting salaries, different healthcare plans, and ultimately leading to one sibling retiring as a millionaire and the other sibling dying young due to limited access to preventative health care through lack of workplace-provided insurance.

The above example helps to demonstrate the complexity of intersectionality, where the classification options are infinite. These challenges and battlegrounds are also illustrated with some of the debates over language. Even within our intersectional classifications, we differ in our choice of terminology. These battles over language are the result of historical hegemonic power structures and are, at times, grounded in foundations of racism and sexism. Changing language preferences in societies revolve around changing power dynamics and are often themselves grounded in where one "sits" in the intersectional spectrum. Language choices are sometimes the results of attempts to walk the neutrality tightrope (i.e. gender-neutral, colorblind, etc.), but this version of neutrality is often a less than subtle way of trying to maintain the status quo and perpetuate systemic and historical inequities (Trochmann, Viswanath, Puello, & Larson, 2022). Failing to account for this new terminology and these trends in reclaiming and reusing language affects organizational crisis management because this constant state of change affords opportunities for recognizing and redressing formerly hidden inequity in staffing, communication, operations, and service delivery from planning to recovery.

This book itself is an example of these challenges and shifting norms, with the various authors and editors having different interpretations of the "right" terminology to be utilized. Table 1.1 illustrates [some] of the differences in language that could be utilized for the various demographic terms throughout this book. Often management demographic terminology

Table 1.1 Intersectionality Terminology Variations

Traditional Terminology	Common Variations	Terminology Used in This Book
Gender	Male/Female (binary), she/her, he/him Sex (binary choice) Sexual Orientation (see also LGBT) Gender identity	Gender - but meaning a range of genders rather than a binary choice
Black/African American	Black, black, African American, Black/African American People of Color Black/Indigenous/People of Color (BIPOC)	Black or BIPOC
LGBT	LGBTQ, LGBTQ+, LGBTQIA+, gay, lesbian, bisexual, transgender, homosexual, cisgender, gender identity, sexual orientation, same-sex, queer	LGBTQ+ in general, other terms when specifically necessary
Hispanic	Hispanic, Latino/Latina, Caucasian/Hispanic origin, LatinX	LatinX

follows US federal terminology such as Census Data or Bureau of Labor Statistics. But alternatively, terminology may also reflect the intersectional nature of the writer as much, if not more, than the intersectional nature of the demographic being discussed. As mentioned in the previous section, choices in language and terminology reflect changing social norms, differences in cultural, racial, economic, regional, and even education or employment differences. Language choices often represent historical dynamics that are interspersed with racism, sexism, homophobia, xenophobia, and hard-fought social justice battles, among countless other influences. We as editors recognize and empower these choices. At the same time, we also recognize the challenges in putting together a project such as this. For the sake of consistency, we have made editorial choices in terminology that will be utilized throughout this book (see Table 1.1) – but we do so with great trepidation because we value what is represented by the wider range of language. The one exception to this will be in Chapter 4 by Hoang et al, where they utilize the language consistent with the official US government sources (i.e. Bureau of Labor Statistics) discussed within their chapter.

Perhaps the most visible of these language battlegrounds in recent decades is centered in racial classifications. Language options begin with the individual racial classifications, but quickly lead to debates and differences. For instance, a seemingly basic racial classification might be "Black" vs. "White." But even the term "Black" could lead to debates and controversy – with some individuals using African American, others prefer-ring "People of Color," and more recently the term BIPOC (Black, Indige-nous, and People of Color) has been utilized. The BIPOC term also overlaps with the acronym AAPI, which stands for Asian American and Pacific Islander. AAPI, which also overlaps with "People of Color" terminology as well as both the Asian and Native Hawaiian/Other Pacific Islander clas-sifications by the U.S. Census, has been a focus of discussion following the increase in hate violence in the US linked to the COVID-19 pandemic. Recently, the *Associated Press* made news when they changed their style guide to capitalize the words such as Black for journalistic writing that is centered in racial or cultural contexts, with this practice intended to convey a shift in inclusiveness, with others seeing this move as a signal of changing power dynamics (Associated Press, 2020).

Older individuals may have been raised using racial terms that are now (quite rightly) considered offensive. Yet these terms are often still present in society completely separate from efforts to move away from the outdated or offensive language. The terms may be present for historical reasons, for example within the name of organizations such as the NAACP, which stands for National Association for the Advancement of Colored People. This organization was founded in 1909 and has been a leader in the bat-tle for civil rights and fighting racial inequality (NAACP, 2022). Despite their name being self-chosen at the founding, there have been major societal changes in terminology over the last century, and perhaps significant debate within their movement, such that the full name of the organization is not uti-lized on the main pages of their own organization's website, only the more recognizable NAACP initials appear.

Changes in terminology are sometimes the result of changing norms in society, representing shifts in power dynamics, and linked to efforts to be more respectful and inclusive. As a counterpoint, terminology, even contro-versial terminology, may continue to be utilized out of preference of those within a group as a reclaiming of power over the terminology. This type of debate over the reclaiming of terminology has been seen in areas such as rap music where words are used in lyrics to describe race and gender that would not be allowed within classrooms, journalism, or to be uttered by those outside of that race (Low, 2007).

Similar battles over reclaiming language and changing societal shifts are seen in connection to LGBTQ+. The last few decades have seen a shift away from derogatory terms (i.e. the "F-word") to LGBT (lesbian, gay, bisexual, transgender), to more current variations recognizing a broaden-ing interpretation of sexual orientation and gender identity (i.e. LGBTQ+). While these changing terms are generally classified as progress, they can also demonstrate the challenges of intersectionality in who has sway over which terms are used (Velasco & Paxton, 2022). Even the LGBTQ+ term could be considered limiting, with others preferring LGBTQIA+, with each initial representing a new recognized identity within the broader classification (LGBTQIA Resource Center, 2022). The changing letters in this term has been described as a visible and intentional recognition of intersectionality within the LGBTQ+ social movement, thereby demonstrating the historical inequities within the "non-cisgender population" (Velasco & Paxton, 2022).

But even the letters of the LGBTQ+ term can be battlegrounds, demonstrated by the letter "Q" – with some identifying the letter for "Questioning" and others defining it as "Queer." The latter term has been an example of previously offensive slurs being reclaimed by some as a sign of empowerment, while others, particularly those of an older generation, may find that term triggering and offensive. At the same time, there are different interpretations of which terms can, or should, be used based upon intersectional categories – such as differences in which terms are utilized depending if you are influenced by governmental classification terms, journalistic practices, or whether you are an academic. For instance, the U.S. Census uses the term American Indian while many within the community use variations of "Native" or "Indigenous." Within journalism, the current practice is to use either the term American Indian or Native Americans, with terminology shifting to First Nation for tribes in Canada and the term Indian restricted to usage in reference specifically to the nation of India (Associated Press Stylebook, 2022). Similar debates revolve around the terms Hispanic, Latino/Latina, regional terms such as Central American, or even variations such as Caucasian/Non-Hispanic. Within academia, terms such as LatinX are being utilized as a sign of recognition and diversity, one that spans to broad differences in terminology and is both inclusive as well as gender-neutral. While these are notable motivations, a recent Pew Research Center report found that only 3% of those within the demographic utilize the term LatinX (Noe-Bustamante, Mora, & Lopez, 2020). Similarly, academia frequently utilizes the word "Queer," as in queer theories or queer studies, despite the differing interpretations of that word within the LGBTQ+ community ranging from empowering, as a reclamation of history, as a form of "critical resistance," or "rejection of normalcy and assimilation" (Langlois, 2017, p. 244), while at the same time being perceived by some as a term of oppression and disrespect (Thelwall, Devonport, Makita, Russell, & Ferguson, 2022).

Clearly, there are complex challenges related to understanding intersectionality and with how best to use this information to guide crisis management. These challenges also raise awareness about the role that informed communication plays within crisis management efforts. A good starting point is to first recognize that terminology and social norms are constantly shifting and evolving. This recognition should enable greater sensitivity to differences to guide key organizational and community actors within crisis management networks. Ultimately, this awareness should lead to a more equitable approach.

Articulating Intersectionality and Crisis Management: A Path to Social Equity

As the reader progresses through this book, the chapters are laid out to frame several key areas of crisis management leadership and to articulate its role in building greater social equity in resilience and recovery. In Chapter 2, Whetstone and Demiroz explore definitions of intersectionality and crisis management, tracing the slow evolution of intersectionality in crisis management scholarship and discussing how this framework can improve resilience in practice. In Chapter 3, Silverio, Montalvo-Liendo, and Carrizales position intersectionality at the center of policy, research, and practice while emphasizing open communication among healthcare stakeholders during crisis. They suggest discourse that is intersectional in nature to transform medical and health education with alternative forms of service delivery to address health inequities. In Chapter 4, Hoang, Cline, and Sabharwal explore human resources management to spotlight the negative impact of workplace disruptions on women during times of crisis. They propose a restructuring of human resources policies and approaches at the Macro, Meso, and Micro levels. The authors also advocate for organizations to employ empathy and relationship building practices to preserve and maintain diversity and inclusion in an effort to advance social equity. In Chapter 5, Diggs, Castillo Krewson, and McCandless examine inequities in the public and nonprofit sector. They explore legal and representative dimensions of intersectionality and demonstrate how statutory, case law, and organizations can promote fairness and justice. They suggest intersectional management strategies to address overlapping inequities in the public and nonprofit sectors during times of crisis.

The remaining chapters articulate how intersectionality and crisis management coexist and interact in networked ways that parallel what Aaron Wachhaus (2012, p. 40) suggests is more of an "anarchist orientation" of "dynamic" interactions among various actors. Preparing for, navigating, and recovering from crisis requires expert, strategic, and integrative management of these various actors and across various network iterations. The ability to effectively manage crisis can be measured in part to the degree with which "whole communities" are fully engaged in planning and managing for it (Hu, Knox, & Kapucu, 2014) and to the degree with which varying intersectional constructs within communities are understood, recognized, and integrated into planning efforts. Kapucu and Hu (2022, p. 8) frame this as a joint crisis response "that enhances the resilience of a community or nation." Consequently, this book asks the reader to consider each chapter's contribution within these conceptualizations that include a networked, inclusive, and intersectional approach of engaging whole communities to best understand what is necessary to be prepared for crisis, before, during, and after the event.

References

Associated Press. (2020, June 20). Associated Press changes influential style guide to capitalize 'Black'. *The Associated Press*. Retrieved from www.theguardian.com/media/2020/jun/20/associated-press-style-guide-capitalize-black

Associated Press Stylebook. (2022). *Race-related coverage*. Retrieved from www.apstylebook.com/race-related-coverage

Atewologun, Doyin (2018). Intersectionality theory and practice. In *Oxford research encyclopedias, business and management*. New York: Oxford University Press.

Blessett, Brandi (2020). Rethinking the administrative state through an intersectional framework. *Administrative Theory & Praxis, 42*(1), 1–5.

Borrego, Espiridion & Johnson III, Richard G. (2017). *Cultural competence for public managers: Managing diversity in today's world*. Boca Raton, FL: Routledge.

Branicki, Layla J. (2020). COVID-19, ethics of care and feminist crisis management. *Gender, Work & Organization, 27*(5), 872–883.

Breslin, Rachel A., Pandey, Sheela, & Riccucci, Norma M. (2017). Intersectionality in public leadership research: A review and future research agenda. *Review of Public Personnel Administration, 37*(2), 160–182.

Bundy, Johnathan, Pfarrer, Michael D., Short, Cole E., & Coombs, W. Timothy (2017). Crises and crisis management: Integration, interpretation, and research development. *Journal of Management, 43*(6), 1661–1692.

Carrizales, Tony, Zahradnik, Anne, & Silverio, Michelle (2016). Organizational advocacy of cultural competency initiatives: Lessons for public administration. *Public Administration Quarterly, 40*(1), 126–155.

Christensen, Tom, & Lægreid, Per (2020). The coronavirus crisis – crisis communication, meaning-making, and reputation management. *International Public Management Journal, 23*(5), 713–729.

Collins, Patricia H. (2019). *Intersectionality as critical social theory*. Durham: Duke University Press.

Crenshaw, Kimberlé (1989). Demarginalizing the intersection of race and sex: A Black feminist critique of antidiscrimination doctrine, feminist theory and antiracist politics. *University of Chicago Legal Forum, 1989*(1), 139–167.

Crenshaw, Kimberlé (1991). Mapping the margins: Intersectionality, identity politics, and violence against women of color. *Stanford Law Review, 43*(6), 1241–1299.

Crenshaw, Kimberlé (2020). 'Difference' through intersectionality 1. In S. Arya & A. S. Rathore (Eds.), *Dalit feminist theory: A reader* (pp. 139–149). Abingdon: Routledge.

Crowder, Chaya & Smith, Candis W. (2020). From suffragists to pink pussyhats: In search of intersectional solidarity. *PS: Political Science & Politics, 53*(3), 490–493.

Dhamoon, Rita K. (2011). Considerations on mainstreaming intersectionality. *Political Research Quarterly, 64*(1), 230–243.

Diggs, Schnequa N. (2022). Intersectionality of gender and race in government affairs. In P. Shields & N. M. Elias (Eds.), *Handbook on gender and public administration* (pp. 115–132). Cheltenham, UK: Edward Elgar Publishing.

Diggs, Schnequa N., Castillo Krewson, Rosa, & McCandless, Sean A. (2023). Intersectional disparities during crisis: Improving social equity through public and nonprofit management. In H. J. Knepper, M. D. Evans, & T. J. Henley (Eds.), *Intersectionality & crisis management: A path to social equity*. New York: Routledge.

Fay, Daniel L., Hicklin Fryar, Alisa, Meier, Kenneth J., & Wilkins, Vicky (2021). Intersectionality and equity: Dynamic bureaucratic representation in higher education. *Public Administration, 99*(2), 335–352.

Gilligan, Carol (1993). *In a different voice: Psychological theory and women's development*. Cambridge, MA: Harvard University Press.

Gilpin, Dawn R., & Murphy, Priscilla J. (2008). *Crisis management in a complex world*. Oxford: Oxford University Press.

Hamidullah, Madinah F., & Riccucci, Norma M. (2017). Intersectionality and family-friendly policies in the federal government: Perceptions of women of color. *Administration & Society, 49*(1), 105–120.

Haupt, Brittany "Brie" (2020). Cultural competency historical presence and development. In C. C. Knox & B. Haupt (Eds.), *Cultural competency for emergency and crisis management: Concepts, theories and case studies* (pp. 26–41). New York: Routledge.

Haupt, Brittany "Brie" & Knox, Claire Connolly (2018). Measuring cultural competence in emergency management and homeland security higher education programs. *Journal of Public Affairs Education, 24*(4), 538–556.

Hoang, Thanh T., Cline, Ravin R., & Sabharwal, Meghna (2023). Women falling through the cracks: Intersectionality during crisis and implications for human resources management. In H. J. Knepper, M. D. Evans, & T. J. Henley (Eds.), *Intersectionality & crisis management: A path towards social equity*. New York: Routledge.

Hu, Qian, Knox, Claire Connolly, & Kapucu, Naim (2014). What have we learned since September 11, 2001? A network study of the Boston marathon bombings response. *Public Administration Review, 74*(6), 698–712.

Hutter, Bridget M., & Lloyd-Bostock, Sally (2013). Risk, interest groups and the definition of crisis: The case of volcanic ash: Risk, interest groups and the definition of crisis. *The British Journal of Sociology, 64*(3), 383–404.

Jashinsky, Terri L., King, Carrie L., Kwiat, Noel M., Henry, Brittney L., & Lockett-Glover, Alexis (2021). Disability and COVID-19: Impact on workers, intersectionality with race, and inclusion strategies. *The Career Development Quarterly, 69*(4), 313–325.

Kapucu, Naim & Hu, Qian (2022). An old puzzle and unprecedented challenges: Coordination in response to the COVID-19 pandemic in the US. *Public Performance & Management Review*, 1–26.

Klobus, Zoë, Evans, Michelle D., & Knepper, Hillary J. (2022). Gender and public administration scholarship. In P. Shields & N. M. Elias (Eds.), *Handbook on gender and public administration* (pp. 364–384). Cheltenham, UK: Edward Elgar Publishing.

Knepper, Hillary J., Scutelnicu, Gina, & Tekula, Rebecca (2020). The slippery slope: Struggling for equity in the academy in the era of #metoo. *Public Administration Review, 80*(6), 1111–1117.

Knox, Claire Connolly, Goodman, Doug, Entress, Rebecca M., & Tyler, Jenna (2022). Compounding disasters and ethical leadership: Case studies from Louisiana and Texas. *Public Integrity (ahead-of-print)*, 1–19.

Langlois, Anthony J. (2017). Queer rights? *Australian Journal of International Affairs, 71*(3), 241–246.

LGBTQIA Resource Center. (2022). *LGBTIA resource center glossary*. Retrieved from https://lgbtqia.ucdavis.edu/educated/glossary

Low, Bronwen E. (2007). Hip-hop, language, and difference: The N-word as a pedagogical limit-case. *Journal of Language, Identity & Education, 6*(2), 147–160.

Marks, Rachel, & Rios-Vargas, Merarys (2021). *Improvements to the 2020 census race and hispanic origin question designs, data processing, and coding procedures.* Retrieved from www.census.gov/newsroom/blogs/random-samplings/2021/08/improvements-to-2020-census-race-hispanic-origin-question-designs.html

Mitroff, Ian, & Alpaslan, Can (2020). *Swans, swine, and swindlers: Coping with the growing threat of mega-crises and mega-messes.* Stanford, CA: Stanford University Press.

Moon, Jukrin, Sasangohar, Farzan, Son, Changwon, & Peres, S. Camille (2020). Cognition in crisis management teams: An integrative analysis of definitions. *Ergonomics, 63*(10), 1240–1256.

NAACP. (2022). *NAACP – our history*. Retrieved from https://naacp.org/about/our-history

Nash, Jennifer C. (2008). Re-thinking intersectionality. *Feminist Review, 89*(1), 1–15.

Noe-Bustamante, Luis, Mora, Lauren, & Lopez, Mark H. (2020). *About one-in-four U.S. Hispanics have heard of Latinx, but just 3% use it.* Retrieved from www. pewresearch.org/hispanic/2020/08/11/about-one-in-four-u-s-hispanics-have-heardof-latinx-but-just-3-use-it/

Pomerleau, Clark A. (2010). Empowering members, not overpowering them: The national organization for women, calls for lesbian inclusion, and California influence, 1960s–1980s. *Journal of Homosexuality, 57*(7), 842–861.

Silberstein, Elodie, Tramontano, Marisa, & Nayak, Meghana V. (2020). *A student primer on intersectionality: Not just a buzzword.* Retrieved from https://digital-commons.pace.edu/oer/3/

Silverio, Michelle, Montalvo-Liendo, Nora, & Carrizales, Tony (2023). Intersectionality and healthcare management: The case of crisis and COVID-19. In H. J. Knepper, M. D. Evans, & T. J. Henley (Eds.), *Intersectionality & crisis management: A path to social equity.* New York: Routledge.

Thelwall, Mike, Devonport, Tracey J., Makita, Meiko, Russell, Kate, & Ferguson, Lois (2022). Academic LGBTQ+ terminology 1900–2021: Increasing variety, increasing inclusivity? *Journal of Homosexuality*, 1–25.

Tomsett, Danny (2020). *What does 'the new normal' mean for business anyway?* Retrieved from www.forbes.com/sites/forbestechcouncil/2020/08/11/what-does-the-newnormal-mean-for-business-anyway/?sh=6f52459526a5

Trochmann, Maren B., Viswanath, Shilpa, Puello, Stephanie, & Larson, Samantha J. (2022). Resistance or reinforcement? A critical discourse analysis of racism and anti-Blackness in public administration scholarship. *Administrative Theory & Praxis*, *44*(2), 158–177.

U.S. Census Bureau. (2022). *About the topic of race.* Retrieved from www.census.gov/topics/population/race/about.html

Velasco, Kristopher, & Paxton, Pamela (2022). Deconstructed and constructive logics: Explaining inclusive language change in queer nonprofits, 1998–2016. *American Journal of Sociology*, *127*(4), 1267–1310.

Wachhaus, T. Aaron (2012). Anarchy as a model for network governance. *Public Administration Review*, *72*(1), 33–42.

Whetstone, Crystal, & Demiroz, Fatih (2023). Understanding intersectionality and vulnerable populations: A missing part in building disaster resilient communities? In H. J. Knepper, M. D. Evans, & T. J. Henley (Eds.), *Intersectionality & crisis management: A path towards social equity.* New York: Routledge.

Wright, James E., & Merritt, Cullen C. (2020). Social equity and COVID-19: The case of African Americans. *Public Administration Review*, *80*(5), 820–826.

2 Understanding Intersectionality and Vulnerable Populations

A Missing Part in Building Disaster Resilient Communities?

Crystal Whetstone and Fatih Demiroz

Introduction

Crisis is a widely used term in everyday language as well as in academic research. In a broad sense, it refers to unfavorable changes in the conditions of a system, such as an ecosystem, an economy, or a communication network. Boin, 't Hart, Stern, and Sundelius (2017) offer a more precise definition of crisis in social systems and suggest that in a crisis situation, "a social system – a community, an organization, a policy sector, a country, or an entire region – experiences an urgent threat to its basic structures or fundamental values, which harbors many 'unknowns' and appears to require a far-reaching response" (p. 5). Naturally, crises impacting social systems are more concerning for the broader public and attract more attention.

Impacts of crisis are felt at varying degrees by different people. Often, vulnerable populations (minorities, women, children, people with disabilities, etc.) are impacted more severely by the threats, urgency, and uncertainty caused by crisis than other people (Wisner & Luce, 1993; Fothergill, 1996; Fothergill, Maestas, & Darlington, 1999; Gooden, Jones, Martin, & Boyd, 2009; Jerolleman, 2019). Efforts for managing crisis need to take not only these individual attributes into account, but also consider the differences of these attributes across social groups for building more resilient communities (Gooden et al., 2009; Vickery, 2018; Tierney, 2019; Kuran et al., 2020). To best understand how vulnerable populations are differently impacted compared to non-vulnerable populations, as well as to highlight the myriad differences in levels and types of vulnerability among various vulnerable sectors, there has been a slow movement toward intersectional analysis. Intersectional analysis stems from the concept of intersectionality, which refers to "the interaction of multiple identities and experiences

DOI: 10.4324/9781003184621-2

of exclusion and subordination" of individuals and social groups, which vary along lines of oppression and privilege (Davis, 2008, p. 67). An intersectional approach enables the ability to best understand resilience across vulnerable and non-vulnerable populations.

This chapter will open a window to crisis management and crisis resilience research through the lens of intersectionality theory. We argue that intersectionality is a key theoretical concept for crisis management when people are the focus, as in a human security perspective. We urge that any efforts for assessing resilience of a community or sub-community to crisis should follow an intersectional approach. We explore the concept of resilience in crisis and disaster management, connecting resilience to vulnerability and marginalization by reviewing the origins of intersectionality in the literature. We highlight the slow progress of intersectionality in crisis management and the applications of intersectionality in building resilient communities.

The Concept of Resilience in Crisis and Disaster Management

The concept of resilience has been widely used in many disciplines and it can have different meanings depending on the context and field of study (Demiroz & Haase, 2019). We use Comfort, Boin, and Demchak's (2010) definition of resilience – a social system's capacity to proactively adapt to and recover from unexpected disturbances. To understand the implications of this definition for intersectionality research, we must break it down into its components. In this definition, resilience is a characteristic of a system. Systems consist of agents (e.g., individuals) with different attributes (gender, socioeconomic status, etc.), interactions between agents (i.e., networks), rules that govern the interactions between agents (laws, customs, social norms), populations of agents that share similar attributes (men, women, Black people, LatinX people, etc.), artifacts (roads, buildings), environment (other social systems), and feedback channels that shape the system (Axelrod & Cohen, 2000) (see Table 2.1).

When this definition of resilience is applied to a community, residents of that community would be the agents in this social system. However, not all residents are the same. The race, ethnicity, gender, socioeconomic status, level of poverty, and other social, political, and economic attributes of the residents have a considerable impact on the system outcomes. The interactions of individuals with one another causes social structures within this community to emerge (Sawyer, 2005). Volunteer disaster response groups are emergent social structures commonly observed after disasters (Quarantelli, 1983, 1994; Demiroz & Akbas, 2022). Individuals who are part of

Table 2.1 Linkage Between Complex Systems and Intersectionality Frameworks

Complex Systems Framework	Intersectionality Framework
Agents	Individuals
Agent attributes	Gender, race, ethnicity, religion, socio-economic status
Agent networks	Social capital, access to information and community resources
Rules that govern agent interactions	Laws and social norms that amplify disadvantages
Artifacts	Schools, hospitals, technology, infrastructure, etc.
Feedback loops	Poverty, disenfranchisement, discrimination, and other negative factors create a vicious cycle that deepens these negative conditions especially for the most vulnerable people

large support networks such as church groups or Rotary Clubs are better positioned to access some vital resources such as information for finding a job or expanding their businesses. These network ties are also called the social capital of an individual.

The impact of social capital on different aspects of community life has been well documented by scholars. Putnam, Leonardi, and Nanetti (1993) found stark differences in social capital between communities, thereby impacting civic-oriented behaviors, (dis)trust in government, and in the extreme, the emergence of non-judicial [mafia-type] organizations. Social capital also proved to be impactful before, during, and after disasters as well. For example, the Mary Queen of Vietnam (MQVN) Catholic Church helped the members of the Vietnamese American community access a "unique bundle of club goods" (Chamlee-Wright & Storr, 2009, p. 429) which helped them rebuild and protect their community and through political action afterward. How much social capital can contribute to community life is shaped by rules that govern human interactions (Axelrod & Cohen, 2000).

Rules governing agent interactions can be formal (e.g., property rights, traffic rules, homeowners' association rules), informal (e.g., customs and traditions), or a combination of the two. These rule structures enable or constrain agents' interactions with others and shape the nature of their connections. For example, the relationship between a child and parents is governed by a combination of a set of shared expectations by society and laws that protect family members. However, both the formal and informal rules and how much they shape human interactions varies depending on the context and the agents' attributes. The relationship between parents and children in an Asian family is likely to differ from the parent-children relationship in a LatinX family due to cultural differences between the two families. Likewise, father-son relationships are different than mother-daughter relationships.

Formal and informal rules can apply differently to agents of different attributes depending on social and political context. Alexander (2010), for example, argues that the *war on drugs policies* apply differently to Black and White drug users. Black users face harsher penalties than White users for using the same type of drug: cocaine. The discrepancy in the application of laws between different racial groups creates feedback loops that foster and amplify mass incarceration, poverty, rundown public schools, poor neighborhoods, loss of basic rights such as voting, and disconnection from the rest of society and the political system (Alexander, 2010; Wilkerson, 2020). Alexander (2010) and Wilkerson's (2020) works reveal two other components of complex social systems: artifacts and feedback channels.

Artifacts are the objects that agents interact with in their built, natural, and social environment. Artifacts can be roads, schools, houses, cars, churches, and other social and technical items surrounding individuals in a society. Feedback channels, both positive and negative, introduce input from actors and systems in the external environment and contribute to system outcomes. Positive feedback reinforces system status and amplifies system outcomes. For example, cities experiencing high crime rates are likely to have lower property values. Low property values create lower tax revenue for local governments and school districts, which leads to poor government capacity, underfunded schools, and rundown neighborhoods. This situation pushes property values even lower, which reinforces the system's (i.e., the community) undesirable conditions. Negative feedback, on the other hand, plays a corrective role in the system. Carefully crafted public policy, appropriate funding, and a politically engaged community can play a corrective role in cities struggling with economic problems, crime, failing schools, and poor local government quality. Thus, it is critical that we understand how feedback mechanisms work in communities and how they shape those communities' conditions.

Information is the most critical substance that flows through feedback channels. Agents in a system rely on information for adjusting their strategies for reaching their goals (Axelrod & Cohen, 2000). For a system to be resilient to crisis and disasters, the system needs to adapt to and recover from stressor events. The adaptability of a system depends on its agents' ability to access information and other resources, modify their strategies in the face of dynamic crisis, and change some of the interaction patterns (i.e., network structures) in which they are embedded. For example, risk information plays a crucial role for public agencies, insurance companies, and other businesses for modifying their policies and practices. Lack of such information can create devastating effects for a system. Outdated FEMA flood risk maps failed to inform residents and public officials about flooding risk in the greater Houston area. Thus, most Houstonians living outside of FEMA's outdated flood zones did not have flood insurance (Smiley, 2020).

Unfortunately, even if information flows in a system through feedback channels, not all agents in the system have the same level of access to information and other resources. Agents with stronger social capital and greater access to better artifacts are more likely to recover from disasters and crisis (Chamlee-Wright & Storr, 2009). Agents who have limited social capital, face double standards in the application of formal and informal rules in interactions, and may be caught up within a vicious cycle of poverty and poor artifacts are more likely to lag in recovery after a disaster or crisis. The second group of agents constitute the soft underbelly of communities when it comes to building resilience against stressor events.

To build crisis resilient communities, we need to understand the components (i.e., diverse actors, interactions, rules, artifacts, and feedback loops) of the community of interest. Saja, Teo, Goonetilleke, and Ziyath's (2018) critical review of social resilience literature resulted in a similar resilience framework that is presented in this chapter. Their findings point out five dimensions of resilience: (i) social structure, (ii) social capital, (iii) social mechanisms, competence, and values, (iv) social equity and diversity, and (v) social beliefs, culture, and faith. The remainder of the chapter focuses on vulnerability, marginality, and social equity aspects of community resilience.

Social Vulnerability and Marginality

Marginalization is understood to emerge from "unequal relationships between one or several groups with power, whether economic, political, social or all together, and a minority or non-members of the said group" (Walters & Gaillard, 2014, p. 212). The homeless, the socio-economically disadvantaged, the elderly, those living with disabilities, women and children, as well as ethnic and racial minorities and migrants of all types are typically depicted in crisis management literature as the marginalized and vulnerable (Fothergill & Peek, 2004). What makes these populations marginalized is not only their attributes but also the nature of their interactions with other populations. In other words, the way that these people are treated by the other populations in a society shapes their level of marginalization. For example, a community's decision about inclusivity when building roads, playgrounds, or sidewalks (i.e., artifacts) determines how marginalized people with disabilities may feel. Marginalized individuals are generally understood as the least resilient in recovering from or being prepared for a crisis (Wisner & Luce, 1993; Fothergill, 1996; Peacock, Gladwin, & Morrow, 1997; Walters & Gaillard, 2014).

While it is critical to recognize particular populations in any community as vulnerable and marginalized, we emphasize the point made by Vickery (2018) who argues that there is a homogenization of the categories of those defined as vulnerable and marginalized in crisis and disaster management studies. This matters in terms of risk assessment to building resiliency as homogenization fails to recognize how gender identities and ethnic and racial identities differently impact pre-disaster, disaster, and post-disaster experiences. Only an intersectional analysis can speak to the differences in risk, vulnerability, and marginalization among various individuals and social groups to best assist crisis management scholars and practitioners with crisis management attuned to context.

Crisis management scholars mostly avoided the question of "how society creates the conditions in which people face hazards differently" (Wisner, Blaikie, Cannon, & Davis, 2004 [1994], p. 10) until the recognition of vulnerabilities of individuals and groups being the result of political choices. Recognizing that vulnerability is a political outcome has enabled scholars and policymakers to engage (if they so choose) in more effective planning for crisis and disasters to anticipate the greater needs for vulnerable and marginalized populations in any given community (Gooden et al., 2009; Domingue & Emrich, 2019; Leach & Rivera, 2021).

Yet, there remains limited scholarly attention to the differences among vulnerable populations based on intersecting oppressions and avenues of power (Vickery, 2018; Kuran et al., 2020). Nevertheless, in a hopeful sign, growing numbers of crisis and disaster management scholars have begun calling attention to the problem of homogenization of vulnerable populations, noting that homogenization results in inaccurate and/or incomplete understandings and assessments that ultimately hinder resiliency building. These studies call for the application of intersectional analysis to aid in crisis and disaster programming to ensure that crisis management is as effective as possible (Vickery, 2018; Prohaska, 2020; Andharia, 2020a; Kuran et al., 2020).

Vulnerable Populations in Crisis and Disasters

When recovering from a disaster or crisis, agents can be at a disadvantage due to two factors: (i) their attributes, and (ii) their connections (networks). The first factor creates vulnerable populations in a social system/community. Finch, Emrich, and Cutter (2010) provide a comprehensive definition of vulnerability and define the term vulnerability as "socioeconomic characteristics that influences a community's ability to prepare, respond, cope, and recover from a hazard event" (Finch et al., 2010, p. 181). More specifically, Cutter and Finch (2008) point out individuals' race, ethnicity, sex, socioeconomic status, age, migration, and housing conditions as sources of vulnerability. Fothergill and Peek's (2004) review of the sociological literature found similar results. They found that individuals' socioeconomic statuses are an important predictor of how well individuals prepare for and recover from disasters. The poor are more likely to live in high-risk areas, engage in risky behavior, ignore warnings, incur material losses, and experience physiological and psychological trauma (Fothergill & Peek, 2004). The role of poverty and other individual attributes (e.g., race) were salient before and after Hurricane Katrina. During Katrina, most of the people who could not evacuate New Orleans were Black and poor. Limited access to transportation made staying in the city the only option for many poor residents. Furthermore, those who stayed in the city faced unnecessary challenges and administrative burdens posed by public administrators due to their race before, during, and after the storm (Stivers, 2007).

The second factor that puts agents at a disadvantage while recovering from disasters and crisis is their connections and interactions with other agents and populations. How connections and interactions between agents and populations are established and practiced can give rise to the marginalization of certain people or populations (Leach & Rivera, 2021). Intersectionality lens helps researchers and policy makers see the impact of these interactions in building crisis resilient communities.

Origins of Intersectionality in Disasters

Intersectionality research has its roots in the feminist literature. Neumayer and Plümper's (2007) groundbreaking comparative analysis indicates that in societies where women hold higher status, women are less disadvantaged in disasters compared to women living in societies in which women have lower social status. The gendered nature of disasters created the sub-area of crisis management known as gender and disaster studies. Gender and disaster studies literature considers gender in "disaster planning, management and research," initially through gender mainstreaming (Cupples, 2007, p. 155). Gender mainstreaming was developed to understand gendered policy impacts and to rectify gender inequitable outcomes (Squires, 2005). It brings in "equal opportunities, equal treatment, women's perspectives, gender, gendered perspectives or, more recently, diversity" into research and/ or policymaking to ensure equal outcomes (Squires, 2005, p. 368). Over the 1990s, gender mainstreaming, which requires working within state and intergovernmental institutions such as the UN, was a favored approach both nationally and internationally to create feminist outcomes (Squires, 2005; Walby, 2011).

Gender mainstreaming was an important step forward in understanding women's situations in disasters, which had historically been understudied. However, only by engaging in a broader assessment of gender in relation to other systemic factors (such as race, class, sexual orientation, ability/ (dis)ability and otherwise) can a more complete understanding of women's experiences in disaster emerge. As these insights developed in gender and disaster, this has influenced crisis management, which in the early 1990s was starting to recognize that the broad category of "the vulnerable" could not be understood in full without breaking down differences among marginalized groups.

Disaster management scholars and practitioners too often view those outside of the hegemonic majority in homogenous terms that ignores the diversity within racial and ethnic minority communities. Black feminist scholars recognized early on that analyzing vulnerabilities one at a time "race *or* class *or* gender" overlooks how these issues intersect for many (Jacobs, 2019, p. 29, emphasis in original; Collins, 1990). Black women in the US – typically impacted by racism, classism, and sexism – have shared issues with the broader Black community but also endure specific, overlapping, and compounding oppressions as Black women (Ransby, 2006; Jacobs, 2019). For example, in 2005's Hurricane Katrina, Black women were more likely than other demographics to be poor, with many unable to leave the city due to lack of resources – a raced and classed issue. Many carried sick and elderly family members in water that reached chest level to get their families to safety. Black women not only had fewer resources compared to others but greater caring responsibilities (Ransby, 2006).

Given the links between sex, gender, and sexuality, scholars of gender and disaster studies have also raised awareness of the particular challenges faced by sexual and gender minorities (also termed members of the lesbian, gay, bisexual, trans, queer, and intersex, or LGBTQ+ community). Dominey-Howes, Gorman-Murray, and McKinnon (2014) argue a critical factor generating vulnerability for those in the LGBTQ+ community is the all-too-common assumption of heteronormativity taken by policymakers working in disaster management. As a result, some relief and recovery programs have harmed those in same-sex relationships. Following Hurricane Katrina, some in same-sex partnerships were resettled in different cities from one another, leading to the breakup of the family. This was because couples were officially defined only in terms of (opposite sex) married couples (marriage equality had not yet been achieved). Such lingering notions may continue to influence many hetero policymakers, making challenging heteronormativity critical.

In addition to considerations of race and sexuality, religious identity and ethnicity also play a role in vulnerability impacting differently situated women in varying ways. Perera-Mubarak (2013) observed that following the 2004 tsunami in Sri Lanka, an ethnically divided country dominated by the majority Sinhalese community – who generally identify as Buddhist – and ethnic minorities encountered different post-disaster situations, even among women living in the same coastal areas where fishing is the predominant occupation of most men. Women were generally tasked with not only the usual household responsibilities but also much of the home-based rebuilding and recovery work in the aftermath of the tsunami because men were typically gone for weeks fishing, the most common way coastal households earn a living. However, women from the Sinhalese majority in coastal communities were able to attend NGO meetings to receive recovery aid, which added to women's workload but also helped these households to make ends meet. For women from the minority Malay community, which practices Islam, women were restricted from attending NGO meetings due to community notions that a woman's place was in the home, which is thought to protect their social status. Malay households, therefore, missed out on some aid since they were unable to travel to obtain the funds.

Such insights have been recognized earlier in gender and disaster studies compared to other sub-areas of crisis management given gender and disaster's connections with broader feminist research. Recent feminist scholarship has increasingly emphasized attunement to differences among women to improve *all* women's situations through intersectional thinking and applying intersectional analysis (Hankivsky, 2005; Squires, 2005; Dhamoon, 2013; Kendall, 2020). This development in academic feminism has, in turn, influenced understandings of how differently situated people are impacted by a given phenomenon, whether that is armed conflict (Hagen, 2016; K.C. and Van Deer Haar, 2019), accessing birth control and raising children (Ross & Solinger, 2017) or enduring domestic violence (Nixon & Humphreys, 2010).

Intersectionality in Crisis and Disasters

Intersectionality is arguably the most significant contribution of feminist scholarship (Davis, 2008). As a political mechanism, feminism is dedicated to social justice and empowerment, although there is a diversity of "feminisms," or approaches to understanding and acting on feminist precepts (Dhamoon, 2013). The roots of intersectionality trace to Black feminists in the U.S. experiencing double jeopardy as both women and Black persons, or the triple oppression of gender, race, and class as a socioeconomically disadvantaged Black woman (Beal, 1970; Lynn, 2014). Kimberlé Crenshaw

(1989) – a Black feminist legal scholar – coined intersectionality in the late 1980s to capture the multiplicity of identity. Intersectionality has transformed feminist scholarship from the 1990s onward, which today generally attends to the differences among women. How women experience sexism depends on all facets of their identities, such as whether they are from the global South, identify as part of an ethnic or racial out-group, or fall beyond heteronormativity (Davis, 2008; Dhamoon, 2013).

Although intersectionality is heralded and used across the social sciences and humanities, it has been critiqued for its lack of conceptual clarity (McCall, 2005; Davis, 2008). Yet, it is the ambiguity and variety of approaches to the uses, methods, and constructions of intersectionality that make this concept a useful scholarly tool to inspire "complexity" and "creativity . . . to raise new questions and explore uncharted territory" (Davis, 2008, p. 79). Intersectionality sheds light on differences among and within various populations of society. For this reason, intersectionality can assist crisis management scholars and practitioners to better assess risk and promote resiliency in crisis and disaster preparation by explicating differences among various sectors of the so-called vulnerable and marginalized.

In the early 1990s, when Crenshaw's work on intersectionality was not yet widely known, Wisner and Luce (1993) contributed to what is tantamount to intersectional analysis, although they did not mention intersectionality. Wisner and Luce's (1993) focus was on the need to accurately identify and assess the risk of vulnerable populations, which they noted varied depending on the populations under assessment. Their argument emphasizes the human costs of disasters and how vulnerable populations face more risk than less marginalized groups. Wisner and Luce (1993) also call for the use of "applied vulnerability analysis" to crisis, and go so far as to suggest that "poor women (e.g., class + gender), old, poor, women (age + class + gender), or old, poor, minority women (age + class + ethnicity + gender)" are those who "are most vulnerable" (p. 131). They highlight class, gender, age, ethnicity, and disability as identities that will increase individuals' risk in disasters.

However, beyond the mention of overlapping oppressions, Wisner and Luce (1993) do not carry forward an extensive analysis of how multiple, intersecting, marginalized identities that reflect the embedded structural inequalities would result in varying outcomes for differently situated marginalized groups. Had they done so, this process could have helped to identify not only the divergent and nuanced issues and interests of differently situated vulnerable populations, but also was a missed opportunity to consider where these marginalized groups had particular (and varying) strengths that would be of use to officials and others working to build resiliency in populations and would have been useful in disaster recovery. Most critically, the authors appear to be unfamiliar with the work of intersectionality scholars, which could have helped to develop their thinking even further and refine their concept beyond merely adding an array of signifiers to a person's identity to instead use these insights in changing social conditions to mitigate future disasters by working toward greater equity among vulnerable and non-vulnerable populations.

Nevertheless, the beginnings of an intersectional lens being applied to crisis management were in the making in Wisner and Luce's (1993) article on vulnerability. Their concerns around embedded structural violence and the overlapping forms of marginalization speak to the issues that Crenshaw (1989) and other intersectionality scholars (Cho, Crenshaw, & McCall, 2013) emphasize. This evolution toward intersectionality continued as more crisis scholars recognized that the homogenization of vulnerable populations in managing crisis, emergencies, disasters, and hazards was problematic (Gooden et al., 2009). While it is accurate (and necessary) to point out that vulnerability and marginalization place particular individuals and social groups at greater risk compared to more privileged groups, the blanket term "victim" of a crisis obscures vast differences among vulnerable sectors of society in terms of the impact of crisis (Fordham, 1999) and our ability to fully recover. As Gooden et al. (2009) emphasize, "avoid[ing] a 'one-size-fits-all' emergency management approach" in addressing the needs of vulnerable sectors results in greater effectiveness and efficiency (p. 10).

Applications of Intersectional Approach in Crisis Management

Since the 2000s, there has been a growing area of research in crisis and disaster management for the most vulnerable, with an emphasis on intersectionality (Thomas, Phillips, Lovekamp, & Fothergill, 2013; Tierney, 2019; Andharia, 2020a). Such studies created opportunities to discuss vulnerabilities from a broader perspective by applying an intersectional lens that not only highlights variability among communities but also within communities. Members of a given community – constructed by a shared identity such as religious background, ethnicity, racial identity and otherwise – will share many common experiences that will differentiate members of this community from at least some populations that fall outside of a given community. However, there will also be significant variation within any given community. Only intersectionality can highlight these differences and the relationships among them.

Despite differences among and within vulnerable populations, policymakers and scholars still tend to lean toward an essentialist approach to defining vulnerable groups that render, for example, all women and children as inherently vulnerable when those who fall within these categories are differently resilient. Asking which members of particular vulnerable communities are more and less vulnerable in particular hazards can alleviate this homogenization (Tierney, 2019). Such an approach supports a recent study on four European countries' national vulnerability assessments, including Estonia, Finland, Sweden, and Norway (Kuran et al., 2020). Estonia and Finland marked "pre-defined" social groups such as those living in rural areas as vulnerable while failing to consider the variability among rural residents, such as by class and gender among any number of intersectional lines, leading to a static understanding of social vulnerability that fails to account for lived differences. Conversely, Sweden and Norway respectively take "a dynamic and situation-oriented understanding of vulnerability" and "situational understanding of vulnerability" (Kuran et al., 2020, p. 5). While the elderly typically face challenges, depicting seniors solely as vulnerable inadvertently stigmatizes them. By taking a fluid approach to vulnerability, children, migrants, the elderly, and others are understood as possessing agency since they are not reduced to a single characteristic. This framework acknowledges that vulnerable individuals may be able to contribute to their own solutions (Kuran et al., 2020).

Vickery's (2018) study on unhoused individuals in Boulder, Colorado who experienced the 2013 Colorado floods followed an intersectional analysis to understand the varying kinds and levels of impact of this event on individuals. Vickery (2018) argues that disaster management studies often paint the vulnerable with a broad brush, "without regard for the intersecting traits and contextual factors that result in unequal disaster and environmental outcomes" (p. 136). Persons of color and migrants – especially so-called "undocumented" immigrants – in overwhelmingly white Boulder are (mis)treated as outsiders, but if an individual cannot speak English, they are even more vulnerable compared to the unhoused who understand English. These varying factors impacted how particular unhoused individuals experienced the 2013 floods and how they dealt with recovery.

Many of the unhoused individuals in Vickery's (2018) study asserted that they were better off in the aftermath of the floods compared to their housed counterparts because of being homeless. Using intersectionality, Vickery (2018) uncovered a theoretically important point about how many who suffer from oppression do not lack agency and even view themselves as partially privileged compared to better-off (non-vulnerable) sectors depending on specific situations. This addresses concerns from crisis management scholars about the disempowering aspects of labeling vulnerable societal sectors as "victims" (Cupples, 2007; Cook, 2016; Tierney, 2019). To Tierney's (2019) point that the vulnerable vary in resilience capabilities based on where they are socially situated, the unhoused in Vickery's (2018) study were better equipped to cope with the difficulties in the aftermath of the disaster.

In addition to unpacking the differences among majority and marginalized communities as well as the variation of those who make up various marginalized communities, it is also critical to understand how the context of a crisis influences experiences of vulnerability. Intersectional analysis can shed light on the context itself. Depending on the specific parameters of a given crisis, some aspects of vulnerability will come to the fore, as will some privileges. Attentiveness to contextuality provides a framework to both pinpoint who the most vulnerable are in a given crisis as well as to understand holistically the particular needs and interests of the most vulnerable.

Andharia (2020b) argues that to understand crisis and disasters, their full context must be considered, specifically the "social, cultural, historical, political and ethical" conditions from which a calamity arises (p. 3). She suggests that this can in part be accomplished through intersectionality. She is critical of the "management" in crisis and disaster management, which lacks contextuality, instead applying technical fixes that depoliticize the context of disasters. Because any intervention to address a crisis is inherently political, attending to power relations is critical. Andharia (2020b) suggests that given intersectionality's roots in social justice, this lens can help scholars and practitioners more accurately understand crisis. Furthermore, intersectionality lays the groundwork for radical transformation post-crisis by outlining pre-crisis inequities. As an analytical lens, intersectionality sheds light on the role that legal structures, social norms, and media in interaction with structural oppressions such as colonialism, racism, heteronormativity, and sexism, have on particular intersections of identities of individuals and social groups.

Empirical evidence supports Andharia's (2020b) claim that superior crisis management occurs when intersectionality is applied. Without an intersectional analysis, unsuitable, insensitive and costly mistakes are more likely. During flash floods in August 2010 in India in the Ladakh region (then part of the state of Jammu and Kashmir), mudslides and flooding destroyed nearly 1,500 homes and killed over 200 people. Post-disaster reconstruction was far less effective than it might have been had a context-specific approach been taken. Former residents of flood-impacted areas received new homes, but the homes had Western-style toilets, and the houses were constructed using tin, both factors displeasing to the residents. This "ignorant intervention" meant that long-term recovery was difficult for those impacted by the flash flood. Because the Ladakhi people were unfamiliar with Western-style toilets, people chose instead to relieve themselves in the open, creating unsanitary health conditions (Arora, 2020).

Socio-cultural factors should play a part in any crisis management intervention to ensure effectiveness (Arora, 2020). This is best done by understanding specific struggles around various intersections of gender, class, racial, ethnic, and/or caste coupled with holistically treating victims of a crisis by providing for their needs outside the reason for intervention. This goes a long way to ensuring resilience (Tsakiridis, 2020; Andharia, 2020c). For instance, Tsakiridis (2020) argues that survivors from West Africa's Ebola virus epidemic – which impacted Guinea, Liberia, and Sierra Leone 2014–2016 – should receive, beyond medical care, material supports to address their compounding needs. Both Liberia and Sierra Leone endured armed conflicts in the 1990s and 2000s that influenced the parameters of the Ebola outbreak, specifically with widespread economic issues. Providing a mattress, cell phone, condoms, and multivitamins as well as ongoing counseling to Ebola survivors provides for the complete needs of the person and helps the local economy (Tsakiridis, 2020).

Putting Pieces Together

This chapter's goal is to bridge the crisis management and intersectionality literatures and discuss how an intersectionality framework can help build disaster resilient communities to stand upon the complex systems framework. That is because resilience is a characteristic of a system and without understanding a system, one cannot make it resilient. By outlining where social inequity and injustice exist, intersectionality, which takes into account the social positionality of individuals and communities as well as the context in which a disaster occurs, allows for (more) effective and efficient crisis management (Gooden et al., 2009; Domingue & Emrich, 2019; Jerolleman, 2019). Without such knowledge derived from intersectionality, aid intended to help communities recover loses the ability to engage with the resiliency communities and fails to address where communities are vulnerable due to inequities (Domingue & Emrich, 2019).

The intersectionality framework connects aptly with the complex systems theory. As presented in Table 2.1, the building blocks of a complex system (Axelrod & Cohen, 2000) can easily translate into concepts used in an intersectionality framework. These concepts can be used for building models of various social systems and exploring potential consequences of policy decisions. Analytical tools such as Agent Based Modeling (ABM) and Social Network Analysis (SNA) are used by scholars for modeling social, economic, environmental, and biological systems extensively (Wilensky & Rand, 2015; Namatame & Chen, 2016). The application of these tools can expand into the intersectionality framework in crisis management and be coupled with qualitative research methods that are widely employed by scholars focusing on intersectionality.

Conclusion

Crises and disasters do not impact everybody in a social system equally. A rich literature on vulnerable and marginalized populations in disaster and crisis management has been developed over the past decades. However, focusing only on individual attributes of individuals (e.g., race, gender, socio-economic status) creates blind spots for researchers and policymakers, which leads to challenges in building resilience. We must understand how multiple attributes (e.g., gender, race, ethnicity, sexuality, religious identity, (dis)ability, class, nationality, caste, trans/cis status, and other points of social location) of individuals and their connections with the rest of society interact with each other. These interactions create additional vulnerabilities that could not be understood focusing only on gender, race, ethnicity, or socio-economic status. Thus, applying an intersectionality lens to crisis management is necessary for minimizing vulnerabilities and marginalization within our communities and building resilience against disasters and crisis. As Jerolleman (2019) asserts, those working in crisis management must ask, resilience for whom? The resilience of any community comes down to the resilience of its most vulnerable members. Using intersectional analysis, crisis management scholars and practitioners can pinpoint where efforts to build resilience are most needed.

We echo Kuran et al.'s (2020) argument that only intersectionality can allow researchers to understand differences within particular social groups and to recognize that vulnerability shifts by contexts – contexts that are themselves dynamic. They stress that "intersectionality becomes a useful perspective to assess vulnerability as a dynamic phenomenon and helps to unveil dimensions of marginalization that are rarely mentioned or not mentioned at all in official surveys and documents" as well as much of crisis management scholarship (p. 5). Kuran et al. (2020) call for engaging in risk assessment that unpacks "an individual's vulnerability along several elements of vulnerability at the same time: a multiplicity and fluidity of elements" (p. 6). We add that assessing individuals' privileges along multiple and varying lines and that understanding where specific people or social groups hold resilience are as important to include in a risk assessment as outlining vulnerabilities.

By unpacking the varying and contrasting strengths and the weaknesses of a given community's vulnerable members, steps can then be taken by crisis management practitioners alongside local government, civil society, and local business actors to create resilient communities by investing in building up the divergent strengths that different vulnerable sectors of society bring to crisis resiliency as well as by addressing the inequities where the marginalized need supports to become more resilient. As discussed, the citizens of a community need appropriate resources to be able to contribute to community networks and for networks to supply information. Both information and resources are what enable communities to adapt in crisis (Axelrod & Cohen, 2000; Comfort et al., 2010). Notably, the strength of community networks benefits the entire community (and vice versa). Communities with multiple strong and inclusive networks are ultimately stronger communities compared to communities with fewer and less inclusive strong networks. This carries implications in practice of how to build up strengths and address the weaknesses of various vulnerable sectors.

Building resilient communities in part entails building up marginalized populations' strengths. To enable the most socioeconomically disadvantaged to be contributing members of their community, these citizens require additional supports. Only when the marginalized can focus attention beyond daily survival can they help contribute to networks that build resilient communities. As we have suggested throughout this chapter, intersectionality provides a basic framework to understand the context in which crisis takes place as well as to highlight the contributions and risk areas of vulnerable populations, which vary in significant ways depending on the marginalized group.

References

Alexander, Michelle (2010). *The new Jim Crow: Mass incarceration in the age of colorblindness*. New York: The New Press.

Andharia, Janki (2020a). *Disaster studies: Exploring intersectionalities in disaster discourse*. Singapore: Springer Singapore.

Andharia, Janki (2020b). Thinking about disasters: A call for intersectionality and transdisciplinarity in disaster studies. In J. Andharia (Ed.), *Disaster studies: Exploring intersectionalities in disaster discourses* (pp. 3–32). Gateway East, Singapore: Springer.

Andharia, Janki (2020c). One size fits all? Polemics of disaster management and development from the perspective of post tsunami experiences of Nicobari Islanders. In J. Andharia (Ed.), *Disaster studies: Exploring intersectionalities in disaster discourse* (pp. 255–284). Gateway East, Singapore: Springer.

Arora, Shubda (2020). 'I lived through a disaster': Disaster memories and lived experiences after that 2010 Leh flash floods. In J. Andharia (Ed.), *Disaster studies: Exploring intersectionalities in disaster discourse* (pp. 107–125). Gateway East, Singapore: Springer.

Axelrod, Robert & Cohen, Michael D. (2000). *Harnessing complexity: Organizational implications of a scientific frontier*. New York: Basic Books.

Beal, Frances M. (1970). Double jeopardy: To be black and female. In R. Morgan (Ed.), *Sisterhood Is powerful: An anthology of writings from the women's liberation movement* (pp. 340–352). New York: Vintage Books.

Boin, Arjen, 't Hart, Paul, Stern, Erik, & Sundelius, Bengt (2017). *The politics of crisis management: Public leadership under pressure* (2nd ed.). Cambridge: Cambridge University Press.

Chamlee-Wright, Emily, & Storr, Virgil H. (2009). Club goods and post-disaster community return. *Rationality and Society, 21*(4), 429–458.

Cho, Sumi, Crenshaw, Kimberlé W., & McCall, Leslie (2013). Toward a field of intersectionality studies: Theory, applications, and praxis. *Signs: Journal of Women in Culture and Society, 38*(4), 785–810.

Collins, Patricia H. (1990). *Black feminist thought: Knowledge, consciousness, and the politics of empowerment*. Boston: Unwin Hyman.

Comfort, Louise, Boin, Arjen, & Demchak, Chris C. (2010). *Designing resilience: Preparing for extreme events*. Pittsburgh, Pennsylvania: University of Pittsburgh Press.

Cook, Sam (2016). The 'woman-in-conflict' at the UN Security Council: A subject of practice. *International Affairs, 92*(2), 353–372.

Crenshaw, Kimberlé (1989). Demarginalizing the intersection of race and sex: A Black feminist critique of antidiscrimination doctrine, feminist theory and antiracist politics. *University of Chicago Legal Forum, 1989*(1), 139–167.

Cupples, Julie (2007). Gender and hurricane mitch: Reconstructing subjectivities after disaster. *Disasters, 31*(2), 155–175.

Cutter, Susan L., & Finch, Christina (2008). Temporal and spatial changes in social vulnerability to natural hazards. *Proceedings of the National Academy of Sciences – PNAS, 105*(7), 2301–2306.

Davis, Kathy (2008). Intersectionality as buzzword: A sociology of science perspective on what makes a feminist theory successful. *Feminist Theory, 9*(1), 67–85.

Demiroz, Fatih, & Akbas, Esra (2022). The impact of social media on disaster volunteerism: Evidence from hurricane Harvey. *Journal of Homeland Security and Emergency Management, 19*(2), 205–243.

Demiroz, Fatih, & Haase, Thomas W. (2019). The concept of resilience: A bibliometric analysis of the emergency and disaster management literature. *Local Government Studies, 45*(3), 308–327.

Dhamoon, Rita K. (2013). Feminisms. In G. Waylen, K. Celis, J. Kantola, & S. L. Weldon (Eds.), *The Oxford handbook of gender and politics* (pp. 88–110). Oxford: Oxford University Press.

Dominey-Howes, Dale, Gorman-Murray, Andrew, & McKinnon, Scott (2014). Queering disasters: On the need to account for LGBTI experiences in natural disaster contexts. *Gender, Place and Culture: A Journal of Feminist Geography, 21*(7), 905–918.

Domingue, Simone J., & Emrich, Christopher T. (2019). Social vulnerability and procedural equity: Exploring the distribution of disaster aid across counties in the United States. *American Review of Public Administration, 49*(8), 897–913.

Finch, Christina, Emrich, Christopher T. and Cutter, Susan L. (2010). Disaster disparities and differential recovery in New Orleans. *Population and Environment, 31*(4), 179–202.

Fordham, Maureen H. (1999). The intersection of gender and social class in disaster: Balancing resilience and vulnerability. *International Journal of Mass Emergencies and Disasters, 17*(1), 15–37.

Fothergill, Alice (1996). Gender, risk, and disaster. *International Journal of Mass Emergencies and Disasters, 14*(1), 33–56.

Fothergill, Alice, & Peek, Lori A. (2004). Poverty and disasters in the United States: A review of recent sociological findings. *Natural Hazards, 32*(1), 89–110.

Fothergill, Alice, Maestas, Enrique G. M., & Darlington, JoAnne D. (1999). Race, ethnicity and disasters in the United States: A review of the literature. *Disasters, 23*(2), 156–173.

Gooden, Susan, Jones, Dale, Martin, Kasey J., & Boyd, Marcus (2009). Social equity in local emergency management planning. *State & Local Government Review, 41*(1), 1–12.

Hagen, Jamie J. (2016). Queering women, peace and security. *International Affairs, 92*(2), 313–332.

Hankivsky, Olena (2005). Gender vs. diversity mainstreaming: A preliminary examination of the role and transformative potential of feminist theory. *Canadian Journal of Political Science, 38*(4), 977–1001.

Jacobs, Fayola (2019). Black feminism and radical planning: New directions for disaster planning research. *Planning Theory, 18*(1), 24–39.

Jerolleman, Alessandra (2019). *Disaster recovery through the lens of justice.* Cham: Springer International Publishing.

K.C, Luna & Van Der Haar, Gemma (2019). Living Maoist gender ideology: Experiences of women ex-combatants in Nepal. *International Feminist Journal of Politics, 21*(3), 434–453.

Kendall, Mikki (2020). *Hood feminism: Notes from the women that a movement forgot.* New York: Viking.

Kuran, Christian H. A., Morsut, Claudia, Kruke, Bjørn I., Krüger, Marco, Segnestam, Lisa, Orru, Kati, . . . Torpan, Sten (2020). Vulnerability and vulnerable groups from an intersectionality perspective. *International Journal of Disaster Risk Reduction, 50*, 1–8.

Leach, Kirk, & Rivera, Jason D. (2021). Dismantling power asymmetries in disaster and emergency management research: Another argument for the application of critical theory. *Risk, Hazards & Crisis in Public Policy*, 1–19. doi:10.1002/rhc3.12243.

Lynn, Denise M. (2014). Socialist feminism and triple oppression: Claudia Jones and African American women in American communism. *Journal for the Study of Radicalism, 8*(2), 1–20.

McCall, Leslie (2005). The complexity of intersectionality. *Signs: Journal of Women in Culture and Society, 30*(3), 1771–1800.

Namatame, Akira, & Chen, Shu-Heng (2016). *Agent-based modeling and network dynamics.* Oxford: Oxford University Press.

Neumayer, Eric, & Plümper, Thomas (2007). The gendered nature of natural disasters: The impact of catastrophic events on the gender gap in life expectancy, 1981–2002. *Annals of the Association of American Geographers, 97*(3), 551–566.

Nixon, Jennifer, & Humphreys, Cathy (2010). Marshalling the evidence: Using intersectionality in the domestic violence frame. *Social politics, 17*(2), 137–158.

Peacock, Walter G., Gladwin, Hugh, & Morrow, Betty H. (1997). *Hurricane Andrew: Ethnicity, gender, and the sociology of disasters*. New York, NY: Routledge.

Perera-Mubarak, Kamakshi N. (2013). Positive responses, uneven experiences: Intersections of gender, ethnicity, and location in post-tsunami Sri Lanka. *Gender, Place and Culture: A Journal of Feminist Geography, 20*(5), 664–685.

Prohaska, Ariane (2020). Still struggling: Intersectionality, vulnerability, and long-term recovery after the Tuscaloosa, Alabama USA tornado. *Critical Policy Studies, 14*(4), 466–487.

Putnam, Robert D., Leonardi, Robert, & Nanetti, Raffaella (1993). *Making democracy work: Civic traditions in modern Italy*. Princeton, NJ: Princeton University Press.

Quarantelli, Enrico L. (1983). *Emergent behavior at the emergency time periods of disasters* (RJ Project 763270/714847). Retrieved from https://udspace.udel.edu/handle/19716/1204?show=full

Quarantelli, Enrico L. (1994). *Emergent behaviors and groups in the crisis time of disasters* (Preliminary Paper). Retrieved from https://udspace.udel.edu/handle/19716/591?show=full

Ransby, Barbara (2006). Katrina, black women, and the deadly discourse on black poverty in America. *Du Bois Review: Social Science Research on Race, 3*(1), 215–222.

Ross, Loretta, & Solinger, Rickie (2017). *Reproductive justice: An introduction*. Oakland, CA: University of California Press.

Saja, A. M. Aslam, Teo, Melissa, Goonetilleke, Ashantha, & Ziyath, Abdul M. (2018). An inclusive and adaptive framework for measuring social resilience to disasters. *International Journal of Disaster Risk Reduction, 28*, 862–873.

Sawyer, R. Keith (2005). *Social emergence: Societies as complex systems*. Cambridge: Cambridge University Press.

Smiley, Kevin T. (2020). *Outdated and inaccurate, FEMA flood maps fail to fully capture risk*. Retrieved from https://kinder.rice.edu/urbanedge/2020/09/30/flooding-Harvey-outdated-and-inaccurate-fema-flood-maps-fail-capture-risk

Squires, Judith (2005). Is mainstreaming transformative? Theorizing mainstreaming in the context of diversity and deliberation. *Social Politics: International Studies in Gender, State & Society, 12*(3), 366–388.

Stivers, Camilla (2007). "So poor and so Black": Hurricane Katrina, public administration, and the issue of race. *Public Administration Review, 67*(S1), 48–56.

Thomas, Deborah S. K., Phillips, Brenda D., Lovekamp, William E., & Fothergill, Alice (2013). *Social vulnerability to disasters* (2nd ed.). Boca Raton, FL: CRC Press, Taylor and Francis Group.

Tierney, Kathleen (2019). *Disasters: A sociological approach*. Cambridge: Polity Press.

Tsakiridis, Alex (2020). Reintegrating the 'other' challenges of stigmatization in policies and practice: The case of Ebola survivors and their relatives during the 2014–2016 epidemic. In J. Andharia (Ed.), *Disaster studies: Exploring intersectionalities in disaster discourse* (pp. 187–211). Gateway East, Singapore: Springer.

Vickery, Jamie (2018). Using an intersectional approach to advance understanding of homeless persons' vulnerability to disaster. *Environmental Sociology, 4*(1), 136–147.

Walby, Sylvia (2011). *The future of feminism*. Cambridge: Polity Press.

Walters, Vicky, & Gaillard, J. C. (2014). Disaster risk at the margins: Homelessness, vulnerability and hazards. *Habitat International, 44*, 211–219.

Wilensky, Uri, & Rand, William (2015). *An introduction to agent-based modeling: Modeling natural, social, and engineered complex systems with NetLogo*. Cambridge, MA: MIT Press.

Wilkerson, Isabel (2020). *Caste: The origins of our discontents*. New York: Random House.

Wisner, Ben, Blaikie, Piers, Cannon, Terry, & Davis, Ian (2004). *At risk: Natural Hazards, people's vulnerability and disasters* (2nd ed.). New York, NY: Routledge.

Wisner, Ben, & Luce, Henry R. (1993). Disaster vulnerability: Scale, power and daily life. *GeoJournal, 30*(2), 127–140.

3 Intersectionality and Healthcare Management

The Case of Crisis and COVID-19

Michelle Silverio, Nora Montalvo-Liendo, and Tony Carrizales

Introduction

National health agencies, politicians, health advocates, and researchers have recognized the persistent existence of health disparities and the urgency to eliminate these disparities (Weber & Parra-Medina, 2003). Health disparities are driven by social (e.g., gender, culture, neighborhood) and economic (e.g., education and income) inequalities (Bowleg, 2021). Managing healthcare with an aim toward equitable services is not a new concept in practice (Carrizales, Zahradnik, & Silverio, 2016). Expectations relevant to culturally competent services can be found in practice as early as the 1800s; however, by the 1980s, there was a collective effort to promote equitable and culturally responsive service by practitioners in health and social services (Satterwhite, Fernandopulle, & Teng, 2007).

Healthcare organizations are committing human and financial resources to address the social determinants of health of their members to achieve health equity. In parallel, private and public payers incrementally support reimbursement models to support healthcare organization efforts (Artiga & Hinton, 2018). However, a longstanding commitment to equity does not automatically translate into equitable services. The limitations and challenges of addressing health disparities can, in part, be attributed to the historically limiting approaches toward the study and practice of healthcare that fail to account for the intersectionality of patients of the communities served and within health care institutions. The following chapter will look at healthcare management from a perspective of intersectionality including a framework to mitigate health disparities during the COVID-19 pandemic.

Intersectionality

Social equity in service-oriented fields has traditionally worked toward assessing services' impact on race, class, and gender. Traditional research

DOI: 10.4324/9781003184621-3

focusing on equity has assumed such underrepresented groups to be independent demographic variables. Intersectionality, on the other hand, "calls attention to the experiences of multiplicatively oppressed groups and the interactivity of social identity structures with a view to radicalizing diversity research, marketing, and advocacy." (Gopaldas, 2013, p. 93). As Bearfield (2009) points out, the future of social equity may very well lie in "questions that address the intersection of race and gender as opposed to approaches that deal with them as separate categories" (p. 382–383). As Young et al. (2020) note, intersectionality is a useful lens to understand how inequities develop and are experienced. Intersectionality embraces the different components of a person's lived experience beyond the sum of an individual's identities (Bowleg, 2021).

As an area of research and practice, intersectionality was advanced by the work of Kimberlé Crenshaw (1989), which critically looked at single-axis frameworks that contribute to the marginalization of black women in feminist theory and anti-racist politics. There was a call for the development of language critical of the dominant view, such as *intersectionality*. Crenshaw (1991) noted how systems of race, gender, and class converge in the experiences of battered women of color and "intervention strategies based solely on the experiences of women who do not share the same class or race backgrounds will be of limited help to women who because of race and class face different obstacles." (p. 1246). Gopaldas (2013) states that the concept of intersectionality refers to the interactivity of social identity structures in fostering life experiences, "especially experiences of privilege and oppression" (p. 90). Ultimately, these experiences founded on intersections of different social locations and power relations lead to inequities (Hankivsky, 2014). Crenshaw's work on domestic violence underscored how intersectionality might be more broadly applicable. These early seminal works aimed at advancing intervention strategies for battered women have since expanded to a field of study that aims at reassessing strategies in various service-oriented areas.

The central ideas of intersectionality are deeply rooted in the United States where complex factors and processes shape human lives and have allowed Black activists and feminists, LatinX, LGBTQ+, and Indigenous scholars to produce important work in the field (Hankivsky, 2014). Collins and Bilge (2016) define intersectionality as "a way of understanding and analyzing the complexity in the world, in people, and human experiences" (p. 2). To this end, intersectionality serves as an analytic tool allowing for the complexity of the world to be better understood (McCall, 2005; Collins & Bilge, 2016). The historical limitations of clinical and population surveys tend to overlook or disregard altogether poor and working-class women of color, consequently lacking any in-depth disparities studies (Weber & Parra-Medina, 2003; Agénor, 2020).

Intersectionality in Healthcare

Intersectionality praxis can help facilitate equitable health policies and practices. As Young, Ayiasi, Shung-King, and Morgan (2021) suggest, applying an intersectional lens to health systems provides a more "nuanced and robust way to examine health inequities" (p. 2). They further note that failing to use an intersectional lens can result in limited analysis of inequity that is focused on outcomes rather than root causes of the inequity (Young et al., 2020). Bowleg (2012) argues that addressing the intersectionality of marginalized groups is considered an essential public health crisis of our time (p. 89). As Hankivsky and Christoffersen (2008) point out, health inequities that are reduced to any single social determinant are inadequate. In order to better understand the dimensions that factor into the social positions and power relations associated with health disparities, intersectionality must be part of the conceptual equation. Furthermore, Hankivsky and Christoffersen (2008) suggest that intersectionality does not simply add social categories to one another in an attempt to understand diverse experiences. Instead, the intersectional paradigm looks at the convergence of health-related experiences, including discrimination and oppression. Utilizing an intersectional approach allows for a better understanding of health inequities and a more accurate and inclusive knowledge of health needs – while also leading to socially just health systems and policies (Hankivsky & Christoffersen, 2008).

An intersectional paradigm in healthcare has resulted in numerous studies that take a deeper look at health inequities among various groups and specific health issues. For example, Himmelstein, Puhl, and Quinn's (2017) work focuses on the experiences of weight stigma at the intersection of race and gender and those disproportionately affected by obesity. Viruell-Fuentes, Miranda, and Abdulrahim's (2012) study on immigrant populations found that cultural markers alone were insufficient in explaining social and health inequities. Viruell-Fuentes and colleagues (2012) argued for a shift from individual culture-based frameworks to an intersectional approach. In a study of Black gay, bisexual men and HIV disparities, Quinn (2019) found that intersectionality provides the needed context to understand behaviors and circumstances that contribute to HIV disparities. Wesp, Malcoe, Elliott, and Poteat's (2019) study on transgender health inequities state that when power structures go unacknowledged, they help further exacerbate structural injustices. Intersectionality, instead, can help move the healthcare field toward an agenda of health justice (Wesp et al., 2019).

Hassiotis (2020) notes how in the study of mental disabilities, there are still major gaps in understanding the impact of ethnicity and race. The study of people with intellectual and developmental disabilities must account for intersectionality to adequately provide the necessary services for marginalized or diverse populations. Moreover, the conceptualization of race goes beyond the existing definitions used in health studies. López, Vargas, Juarez, Cacari-Stone, and Bettez (2018) looked at mental health and suggested three multidimensional measures of race. They propose (i) "street race," or how you believe other "Americans" perceive your race at the level of the street; (ii) socially assigned race, and (iii) "self-perceived race." They argue that by expanding on the concept of race, social inequalities can be better understood. Intersectional inquiry of street race and gender finds that only self-perceived race correlates with physical health and that street race is associated with mental health (López et al., 2018).

Intersectional praxis in healthcare underscores the importance of acknowledging patients' multiple demographics and the implications for treatment. Cho (2019) suggests an intersectional framework can be used in accurately diagnosing patients to help address "systematic issues of symptom minimization and diagnostic overshadowing for patients who face discrimination, marginalization, or disparities in the healthcare system" (Cho, 2019, p. 4). Research shows that there are various intersectionality frameworks that have been developed and can serve as a resource for healthcare policies and management and are continuously being explored.

In quantitative population health studies, methodological approaches other than multilevel modeling are needed to truly get at the intersectionality's fundamental ideal of addressing inequities (Agénor, 2020). As Bauer (2014) points out, intersectionality offers health studies a more precise identification of inequalities and in turn, develops necessary intervention strategies designed for specific communities. Focusing on intersectional issues can also help reduce bias and avoid threats to construct validity "by identifying whether identity, position, process or policy variables are relevant, and thus avoiding inadvertent use of proxy variables" (Bauer, 2014, p. 15). Intersectionality research has historically focused on exploring the intersecting relationships among race, class, and gender. However, additional intersecting frameworks of religion, spirituality, culture, geography, place, and age have emerged in research and study to underscore their role in healthcare policy and practice (Hankivsky, 2012; Henley & Boshier, 2016).

López and Gadsden (2016) indicate that "critical, self-reflexive intersectionality health equity lens and praxis depend upon a visceral commitment to uncovering the workings of the multiple systems of inequality in unpacking the social determinants of health" (p. 8). Healthcare structures must be willing to commit to addressing the health inequities through policy and praxis and develop the necessary frameworks that ask critical questions. Caiola, Docherty, Relf, and Barroso (2014) note that acknowledging social determinants in producing health inequities by the scientific community alone has not necessarily translated into significant progress toward interventions. Intersectional praxis and inquiry that matches the complexity of social forces shaping inequities is a necessary advancement in healthcare structures (Caiola et al., 2014; Wilson, White, Jefferson, & Danis, 2019; Bowleg, 2021).

Healthcare Workers

Identifying and studying multiple intersecting dimensions is a challenging area of research; however, as Hankivsky (2012) underscores, the hard work reinforces how these new ways frame the complexity of people and existing social inequities. To this end, Hankivsky (2012) has outlined a guide that can help navigate intersectional research. The guide includes questions based on literature sources that ask general research questions (e.g. Who is being studied? and Who is being compared to whom?). Additionally, the questions also address whether the research is framed within the current cultural, political, economic, societal, and/or situational context; where possible, does it reflect the self-identified needs of affected communities? The guided questions also look at the experiences of diverse groups, power structures, and patterns of inequality that aim to establish a research study that allows for in-depth intersectional understandings (Hankivsky, 2012). These intersectional understandings help further research when assessing the healthcare workforce.

Inequalities in the American workforce include the healthcare sector where healthcare workers were faced with extraordinary stressors during the COVID-19 crisis. Richey and Pointer (2021) note that women comprise 76% of the healthcare workforce in the United States and experienced higher psychosocial ramifications during the pandemic due to gender disparities. For example, women who are mothers may be navigating and managing abnormally high parental and occupational workloads (Richey & Pointer, 2021). Furthermore, Samra and Hankivsky (2021) argue that patriarchal cultures in medicine constrain women doctors' career choices while medical textbooks reinforce norms based on Whiteness by under-representing racial and ethnic minorities. They call for adopting an intersectionality framework for dismantling the power structures in healthcare – going beyond focusing on one dimension at a time such as patriarchy or racism.

During the onset of the pandemic, the healthcare workforce encountered aggravated psychological pressure and even mental illness (Vizheh et al., 2020). These added pressures could be compounded for women in healthcare, where the conflation of gender with the requirements of emotional labor results in work skills and abilities that are taken for granted (Guy & Newman, 2004). Burnout, which is associated with anxiety, depression, and substance abuse in healthcare workers was prevalent pre-COVID-19 and the ongoing pandemic has only exacerbated this healthcare crisis (Prasad et al., 2021; Preti et al., 2020).

Healthcare workers faced the death of their colleagues and threats to their lives along with the fear of COVID-19 exposure for themselves or their loved ones (Billings, Ching, Gkofa, Greene, & Bloomfield, 2021). They had to manage the burden of increased personal protective equipment (PPE) and its negative impact on communication with patients (Billings et al., 2021; Vizheh et al., 2020). Healthcare workers also had to manage elevated workloads due to staff shortages (inadequate staffing or absences because of health or caring responsibilities) (Billings et al., 2021). During the COVID-19 pandemic, women, LatinX, and Black healthcare workers were also more likely to report a more challenging work environment and higher stress scores as compared to men and White health care workers (Prasad et al., 2021). To mitigate these adverse outcomes, it is important for healthcare workers to have shared decision-making between front-line workers and senior leadership and for healthcare organizations to prioritize staff safety (Billings et al., 2021). Healthcare organizations must also offer on-site mental health services and training, which can play an important role in allaying health workers' concerns as well as promoting team cohesion and social support (Billings et al., 2021). Overall, viewing healthcare workers through the intersectional lens underscore the race, gender, pay, and socio-economic disparities that impact opportunities for workers during COVID-19.

In addition, management needs the application of an intersectional lens for leadership in healthcare. Specifically, gender intersects with other social stratifiers so as to influence career progression of health systems leaders (Zeinali, Muraya, Molyneux, & Morgan, 2021), similar to the existing gaps in other fields such as nonprofit boardrooms (Women's Nonprofit Leadership Initiative, 2022). With increased calls and focus on the role of women in leadership in healthcare there has been little attention to intersectionality (Zeinali et al., 2021).

Efforts for increasing women in leadership positions in healthcare fall short. Zeinali et al. (2021) argue that these efforts focus mainly on homogeneous attributes and little attention is "paid to other social axes that intersect with gender to inhibit progression to higher level positions" (p. 7). They note that acknowledging intersectionality of gender and social factors helps in avoiding delays in advancing policies and practices that can benefit women from different backgrounds (Zeinali et al., 2021, p. 7).

Implications for Management

Intersectionality as a framework for the study and practice of management requires a reframing of existing practices. As Blessett (2020) notes in the field of public services, "intersectionality is a disruption of the norm" (p. 4). Service-oriented fields must be willing to embrace inclusive perspectives, ideologies, and methodologies to counter the existing marginalization of identities among institutions (Blessett, 2020). There is now an extensive body of literature on intersectionality that allows health sector organizations to build upon. Collins (2019) suggests that there is sufficient scholarship of intersectionality's cognitive architecture allowing for action necessary in fostering social change. Diversity management strategies of the past should move toward taking an intersectional lens toward diversity and organizational management. There is a growing body of critical perspective on diversity management (Dennissen, Benschop, & van den Brink, 2020; Nkomo & Hoobler, 2014; Zanoni, Janssens, Benschop, & Nkomo, 2010). The single contextual framing of identities within diversity management builds on the call for intersectional research and analysis. For example, Dennissen et al.'s (2020) study of diversity network organizations called for international frameworks. They note that diversity networks are in-company networks designed to support employees with similar social identities which could further marginalize members with disadvantaged identities. Intersectional analysis shows the single category structure of diversity networks is hindered by preserving privilege rather than interrogating it (Dennissen et al., 2020).

Communication

Communication is key for organizations in avoiding potential absences of voices and representations in some intersectional experiences (Walker & Muñoz Rojas, 2021). Healthcare organizations must consider the implications of communication within the context of intersectionality. For example, the earliest studies of intersectionality by Crenshaw (1989) looked at the implications of communication on immigrant populations. Crenshaw's past research on domestic violence found that language barriers are a structural problem for non-English-speaking women. Language barriers limited access to necessary information about shelters and the security shelters provide. Similarly, language barriers during the COVID-19 pandemic limited public health prevention messaging and interventions to reach populations with limited English proficiency (LEP) (Macias Gil et al., 2020; Rozenfeld et al., 2020). Organizations committed to ensuring equity analyzed the data and pivoted to address the barriers (e.g., hiring additional interpreters or texting instead of emailing to ensure real-time communication) to reach LEP populations (Diamond, Jacobs, & Karliner, 2020; Sivashanker, Couillard, Goldsmith, Walker, & Eappen, 2020).

In addition, communication must consider the historical context of power dynamics within an organization. As Van Herk, Smith, and Andrew (2011) highlight, acknowledging and responding to the presence of privilege and oppression and the associated power dynamics within healthcare can help to alleviate social injustices that arise from unequal power relations. Shaffner, Mills, and Mills (2019) note the importance of power relations to intersectional history, the study of organizational management must be concerned with "political domination – power and politics impacts how the past is told, preserved, and reproduced in formal settings" (p. 451). Young et al. (2021) argue that "decisions on how health systems are governed, financed and delivered are driven by established governance structures, which are rooted in historical and contemporary systems of oppression and power" (p. 1). To this end, cultural and interpersonal dimensions of power impact the working relationships and communication structures of organizations. Communication is critical in advancing intersectionality by management, especially during times of crisis.

Organizational

Healthcare institutions have an opportunity to invest in more intersectional funded research that will allow for improved healthcare service delivery. Cho (2019) notes how institutions can direct funded research toward identifying underlying causes of misdiagnosis in various, intersectional populations. Organizations, particularly healthcare institutions, have invested in health equity issues by approaching services through cultural competence (Carrizales et al., 2016). However, cultural competence perspectives alone do not necessarily acknowledge intersectional factors and the associated institutional processes contributing to social injustices (Fitzgerald & Campinha-Bacote, 2019). Fitzgerald and Campinha-Bacote (2019) further suggest that the organizational aim of developing a culturally competent healthcare workforce has led to the unintentional focus on shared group characteristics and the undervaluing of intersectionality. They call on an interconnected process of healthcare professionals and healthcare organizations working together and advancing organizational policies, programs, services, and practices that reflect respect, equity, and values for diversity and inclusion. Most notably, at the organizational level, leadership teams "must continuously assess the organization's environment, policies, procedures, knowledge, and skills related to individual work practices" (Fitzgerald & Campinha-Bacote, 2019, p. 1).

Vizheh et al. (2020) have recommended that organizational managers in the healthcare sector take supportive action for healthcare workers. This includes "encouragement and motivational, protective, and training and educational interventions, especially through information and communication platform[s]" (Vizheh et al., 2020, p. 1975). Vizheh et al. (2020) further suggest that it is necessary to address healthcare worker's physical needs, such as access to healthy meals and hydration and regular rest breaks. These require organizational commitment to their workforce. Furthermore, management can consider shorter working hours and rotating shifts especially for those working in high-risk departments, accommodation and lodging for staff working in high-risk areas, and support for childcare needs, all while continually monitoring the physical and mental well-being of healthcare workers in trying to identify staff who are burned-out or have psychological distress (Vizheh et al., 2020). These organizational implications and management strategies, when implemented from an intersectional framework, can help understand the existing disparities among the healthcare workforce discussed, and most notably limit the extent of disparities during times of crisis.

Intersectional Framework

Developing an intersectional framework for healthcare practices must be based on effective communication and organizational reframing. Intersectional research and practices run counter to traditional approaches and guidance. When approaching intersectionality from a research perspective, Corus and Saatcioglu (2015) note the construct as a paradigm. This approach requires questions of consumer participation including appropriate type of intersectionality and the impact of power dynamics. It is critical to incorporate intersectional approaches to determine and discuss practical and policy implications of analysis (Corus & Saatcioglu, 2015). One example of incorporating intersectional analysis is Hankivsky's (2014) "Intersectionality-Based Policy Analysis (IBPA) Framework," which provides a set of guiding principles and questions that can help bring issues of equity to healthcare policy (Hankiivisky, 2014). The IBPA is designed to generate new perspectives about policy issues and affected populations. The IBPA asks about the short-, medium-, and long-term solutions for policymaking to reduce inequities.

As with most intersectional frameworks that have been developed and proposed in varying service fields, the core tenets remain similar. Reframing intersectionality is essential to address health equity adequately.

In our proposed intersectional framework for healthcare management, the first core principle is: to *place intersectionality as the center of healthcare*

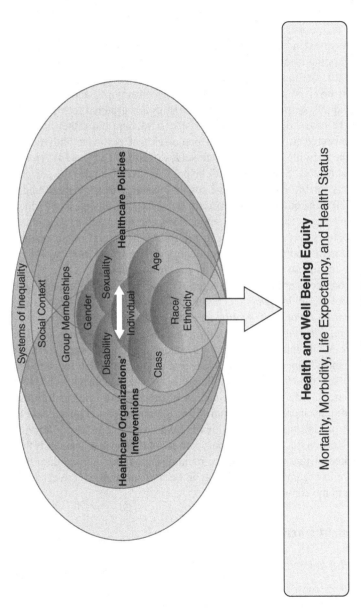

Figure 3.1 Intersectionality in Healthcare Organizations and Policies

Source: Adapted from The Intersection Onion (Bešić, 2020) and Social Determinants of Health (Orgera, Garfield, & Rudowitz, 2021).

research, policy, and practice. Placing conceptual and practical questions of intersectionality at the center of healthcare praxis will help mitigate the marginalization of groups. Moreover, the reframing of intersectionality allows for an emphasis rather than an afterthought in research, policy, and practice. As noted in Figure 3.1, at the core of the onion is the individual and their overlapping identity markers, which is represented by a Venn diagram (Bešić, 2020). The individual is one with all their identities simultaneously. In the next layer of the onion are "Group Memberships" and it signifies how individuals sharing similar characteristics are grouped together. It is important to note "identities do not exist in a vacuum but rather are intimately connected to how the world perceives that particular individual" and how the individual perceives themselves (Bešić, 2020, p. 114). This is represented by the "Social Context" layer. This layer includes the societal expectations for the individual and power dynamics they operated under (Bešić, 2020). The outer layer represents the "Systems of Inequality," which include sexism, racism, religious oppression, ageism, classism, and more (Bešić, 2020). Layered on top are healthcare policies and organizations' interventions to incorporate intersectionality as part of the inner workings to achieve health and well-being equity for their community.

The second core principle of an intersectional framework for healthcare management is: to *implement communication standards that have open communication among all healthcare stakeholders about the importance of individual identities in healthcare research, policy, and practice.* The importance of communication cannot be understated within the context of intersectionality. Open communication that is bi-directional and circular among the key stakeholders in healthcare is critical in advancing intersectional practices. Life experiences and identities that are historically marginalized require increased communication. Communication must come in the form of asking the right questions in healthcare studies and in-service practices. However, it should also be a part of communication standards that openly acknowledge the importance of intersectionality – a standard that is reflective in organizational mission and communicated effectively from leadership to the community.

Management During Crisis

COVID-19 Pandemic and Intersectionality

COVID-19 disrupted lives throughout the world and exacerbated pre-existing inequalities in society. For example, counties with higher COVID-19 mortality rates had a higher proportion of Black residents and greater levels of adverse social determinants of health (i.e., percentage of uninsured adults, percentage of live births with low birthweight, and percentage of adult residents with less than a high school diploma) (Dalsania et al., 2021). Furthermore, women, people of color, and low-income groups experienced a disproportionate burden of risk of the disease, deaths, and social consequences of the safety measures and closures (Mackey et al., 2021; Maestripieri, 2021; Razai, Kankam, Majeed, Esmail, & Williams, 2021). For example, shutdown safety measures disproportionately impacted women in terms of job loss or reduction of working hours to attend to household responsibilities (Matthewman & Huppatz, 2020). Shutdown safety measures were also more likely to disrupt the job market for people of color and low-income groups and result in income loss (Maestripieri, 2021). For people of color and low-income groups that remained in the job market, they were more likely to be at higher risk of exposure to COVID-19 as essential workers (Maestripieri, 2021). In conclusion, COVID-19 differentially impacted segments of the population.

There is a need for a reframed approach and opportunity for healthcare management to address health inequities through an intersectional framework. As Bowleg (2021) points out, intersectionality equity metrics can be beneficial in times of crisis, exemplified through the COVID-19 pandemic. The COVID-19 pandemic impacted vulnerable or marginalized intersections of groups in many areas of healthcare practices, for example, coronavirus testing, contact tracing, vaccine distribution, healthcare policy, allocation of personal protective equipment, healthcare research, and COVID-19 surveillance (Bowleg, 2021). Sekalala et al. (2021) argue that the implementation of human rights law, that can take into consideration intersectional needs, will lend itself to addressing the disproportionate impact that COVID-19 is having on population groups with pre-existing social and medical vulnerabilities. Specifically, Sekalala et al. (2021) note that the existing frameworks/mechanisms and proposals for COVID-19 vaccine allocation could be remedied by adopting an intersectional allocative approach. These approaches could include prioritizing groups historically marginalized in alignment with human rights' needs.

There is a historical precedence of how a pandemic can heighten inequalities in health. Drawing upon international research of the Spanish influenza pandemic of 1918 and the H1N1 outbreak of 2009, Bambra, Riordan, Ford, and Matthews (2020) found socioeconomic, ethnic, and geographical inequalities in infection and mortality rates. Bambra et al. (2020) dispels the myth of COVID-19 "as a socially neutral disease" by noting that just as 100 years ago, inequalities are being magnified because of the pre-existing epidemics of chronic disease (p. 965). Bambra et al. (2020) suggest that COVID-19 exacerbates existing social inequalities in chronic disease and the social determinants of health. Lokot and Avakyan (2020) reflect how historically, the impact of illnesses among gender can be disproportionate. During the Ebola outbreak, women were more exposed to the virus than men because of their funeral rites role that exposed them to infected bodies (Lokot & Avakyan, 2020).

Early studies into the COVID-19 pandemic have underscored the importance of intersectional approaches in healthcare. Ryan and El Ayadi (2020) suggest that the pandemic has been exacerbating existing inequities requiring delineating the heterogeneity of risks to better understand the scope of impact. They find that COVID-19 disaggregated case reports show infection rates are higher for women with greater symptom severity for men. Moreover, Obinna (2021) argues that the COVID-19 pandemic has compounded existing inequalities and vulnerabilities in health issues faced by Black women, such as obesity, diabetes, and hypertension. Obinna (2021) further calls upon targeted policy interventions to help mitigate the effects of COVID-19 and lessen the impact on Black communities.

Reflection upon the early stages of the pandemic and the emergency lockdowns showed numerous examples of unequal health impacts. The unequal experiences of lockdowns were affected by differences in job and income loss, overcrowding, urbanity, access to green space, and critical worker roles as examples (Bambra et al., 2020). In addition, access to healthcare services for non-COVID-19 reasons were limited in stages of the pandemic where health systems were overwhelmed. These limitations in access to healthcare only helped to exacerbate existing inequalities.

Examining the long-lasting impacts of the COVID-19 pandemic would benefit from an intersectional approach to help understand the disruption of health services for marginalized groups. The pandemic may have a lasting effect on women's health via formal and informal health services (Ryan & El Ayadi, 2020). The pandemic lockdowns may also have long-term consequences on mental health and gender-based violence, especially with the existing marginalized groups (Bambra et al., 2020). Moreover, the pandemic and subsequent lockdowns have also led to an increase in domestic violence throughout the world. In turn, care for survivors and access to violence screening through routine health visits are being disrupted through gaps in care (Lokot & Avakyan, 2020; Ryan & El Ayadi, 2020).

Accessibility, availability, and affordability of mental health care overall is a challenge, across the country and particularly for rural communities (Wilson, Bang, & Hatting, 2015). An even bigger challenge exists for women living with violence due to limited financial and social support, fear of deportation, and transportation (Montalvo-Liendo, Page, Chilton, & Nava, 2021). The intersection of poverty and domestic violence existed long before COVID-19. The COVID-19 pandemic created obstacles especially for uninsured or underinsured LatinX women living with violence who need access to free nurse-led support groups that help address their mental health well-being. Nurse-led support groups held in-person provide a safe place for women survivors who are seeking to heal physically and emotionally (Montalvo-Liendo et al., 2021). A virtual platform is a viable alternative to provide the needed support for this population safely; however, the lack of technology and bandwidth for rural and low-income communities is a huge barrier.

As much as Crenshaw raised the call for intersectionality in the study of domestic violence, the COVID-19 pandemic will require a similar approach to research and the practice of healthcare as we move forward. The COVID-19 pandemic has further shown health inequities in the racial disparities among the morbidity and mortality rates (Hassiotis, 2020; Chunara et al., 2021). Moreover, as Chunara et al. (2021) point out, it is not only the outcomes but also the access and equity in care. Healthcare disparities occurred among those needing in-person and virtual services while telehealth increased during the COVID-19 pandemic. Chunara et al. (2021) found that "Black patients were significantly less likely to access care through telemedicine compared to white patients in 2020" (p. 37). Access to sexual and reproductive health services for women has also been found to be inequitable as a result of the COVID-19 pandemic. Lokot and Avakyan (2020) conducted an intersectional analysis to underscore how forms of oppression, inequity, and social and political factors impact sexual and reproductive healthcare during the crisis. Engaging with the marginalized groups affected during the crisis helps ensure their voices and experiences inform the process of sexual and reproductive healthcare access (Lokot & Avakyan, 2020). Engagement and communication become a critical component of managing during a crisis.

Communication during the COVID-19 pandemic crisis is a critical aspect in combating health inequities. Hull, Stevens, and Cobb (2020) note that communication practices are necessary for informing those efforts that can mitigate racial bias and provide guidance in COVID-19 diagnosis, prevention, and treatment in an equitable manner. Communication efforts during times of crisis should provide transparency, especially in the distribution of resources, while also closing information gaps, fighting off misinformation, and helping build trust (Hull et al., 2020). During the height of the pandemic crisis, information on access to care was critical. Access to free meal services and disability services for high-risk families was already facing challenges prior to the pandemic because of limitations to information (Gabrielli & Lund, 2020).

Healthcare management during a crisis should also assess the impact on healthcare workers. By disregarding intersectional perspectives, the risk of not seeing differences and potential factors contributing to the disproportionate number of vulnerability and deaths in the workplace among certain groups increases (Nazareno et al., 2021). As Barello and Graffigna (2020) note – healthcare professionals require enhanced support, enabling them to become aware of their emotions and lived experiences. The authors suggest that an emotional surge related to feelings of burnout can overwhelm the medical system and ultimately impact assessment and action in any healthcare crisis.

In addition, leadership in healthcare requires an intersectional lens and should "take into account other intersecting social identities that create unique positionalities of privilege and/or disadvantage" (Zeinali et al., 2021, p. 1). Zeinali et al. (2021) highlight how there have been calls for women leading the post-COVID-19 pandemic efforts due to their "exemplary leadership of the pandemic response" (p. 7). However, they note that in order to "have more equitable, gender-responsive, and inclusive health systems . . . examinations of gender biases in health system leadership, using intersectional analysis, is needed" (Zeinali et al., 2021, p. 8).

Placing intersectionality at the core of healthcare organizations allows for mitigating the severity of marginalized groups during times of crisis. As Figure 3.2 suggests, when accounting for intersectionality in healthcare

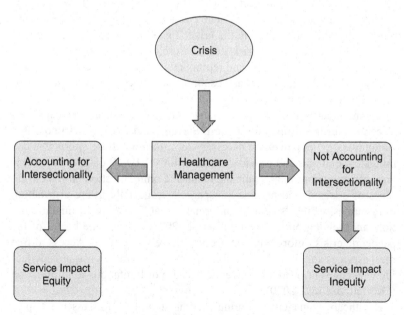

Figure 3.2 Equity Impact when Accounting for Intersectionality in Healthcare Management

management, the degree to which service inequities can occur are reduced. In times of crisis, existing service inequities could potentially be increased and create further distance in the ability of healthcare institutions to provide effective and equitable care.

Conclusion

For healthcare organizations and management to continue the fight against health inequities, the adoption of intersectional approaches in research, education, and practice must be adopted. As Blessett, Gaynor, Witt, and Alkadry (2016) point out, the real world is more complex than typically presented, with respect to disparity and inequity – requiring alternative theories, methodologies, and perspectives. The inclusion of intersectional discourse in healthcare education and the inclusion of alternative approaches in service delivery, such as the prioritization of high-risk families during times of crisis (Gabrielli & Lund, 2020), all lend themselves toward combating health inequities that have persisted for generations.

This chapter has built upon decades of research of intersectionality, to provide a framework for healthcare management. This framework is built off two core tenets that, when adopted, can help historically marginalized groups receive equitable care and help mitigate these disparities during times of crisis.

Principal Tenets of an Intersectional Framework for Healthcare Management

1) *Reframe intersectionality to be viewed as the center of healthcare research, policy, and practice.*
2) *Implement communication standards that have open communication among all healthcare stakeholders about the importance of individual identities in healthcare research, policy, and practice.*

The ability to manage in a time of crisis is most vital when the organization supports individual healthcare workers. This approach requires an interconnected relationship between the healthcare organization, healthcare providers, and healthcare patients. The relationship must be intentionally rooted in an understanding of how an individual's race and gender, as well as other factors, have historically led to healthcare inequities. In order to overcome these inequities, communication and a genuine commitment to address and eradicate healthcare inequity must be acknowledged by those in the service of providing care.

References

Agénor, Madina (2020). Future directions for incorporating intersectionality into quantitative population health research. *American Journal of Public Health, 110*(6), 803–806.

Artiga, Samantha & Hinton, Elizabeth (2018). *Beyond healthcare: The role of social determinants in promoting health and health equity.* Washington, DC: Kaiser Family Foundation. Retrieved from: https://files.kff.org/attachment/issue-brief-beyond-health-care

Bambra, Clare, Riordan, Ryan, Ford, John, & Matthews, Fiona (2020). The COVID-19 pandemic and health inequalities. *Journal of Epidemiology and Community Health, 74*(11), 964–968.

Barello, Serena, & Graffigna, Guendalina (2020). Caring for health professionals in the COVID-19 pandemic emergency: Toward an "epidemic of empathy" in healthcare. *Frontiers in Psychology, 11*, 1431.

Bauer, Greta R. (2014). Incorporating intersectionality theory into population health research methodology: Challenges and the potential to advance health equity. *Social Science & Medicine, 110*, 10–17.

Bearfield, Domonic A. (2009). Equity at the intersection: Public administration and the study of gender. *Public Administration Review, 69*(3), 383–386.

Bešić, Edvina (2020). Intersectionality: A pathway towards inclusive education? *Prospects, 49*(3–4), 111–122.

Billings, Jo, Ching, Brian C. F., Gkofa, Vasiliki, Greene, Talya, & Bloomfield, Michael (2021). Experiences of frontline healthcare workers and their views about support during COVID-19 and previous pandemics: A systematic review and qualitative metasynthesis. *BMC Health Services Research, 21*(1), 1–17.

Blessett, Brandi (2020). Rethinking the administrative state through an intersectional framework. *Administrative Theory & Praxis, 42*(1), 1–5.

Blessett, Brandi, Gaynor, Tia S., Witt, Matthew, & Alkadry, Mohamad G. (2016). Counternarratives as critical perspectives in public administration curricula. *Administrative Theory & Praxis, 38*(4), 267–284.

Bowleg, Lisa (2012). The problem with the phrase women and minorities: Intersectionality– an important theoretical framework for public health. *American Journal of Public Health, 111*(1), 88–90.

Bowleg, Lisa (2021). Evolving intersectionality within public health: From analysis to action. *American Journal of Public Health, 111*(1), 88–90.

Caiola, Courtney, Docherty, Sharron, Relf, Michael, & Barroso, Julie (2014). Using an intersectional approach to study the impact of social determinants of health for African-American mothers living with HIV. *Advances in Nursing Science, 37*(4), 287–298.

Carrizales, Tony, Zahradnik, Anne, & Silverio, Michelle (2016). Organizational advocacy of cultural competency initiatives: Lessons for public administration. *Public Administration Quarterly, 40*(1), 126–155.

Cho, Hae L. (2019). Can intersectionality help lead to more accurate diagnosis? *The American Journal of Bioethics, 19*(2), 37–39.

Chunara, Rumi, Zhao, Yuan, Chen, Ji, Lawrence, Katharine, Testa, Paul A., Nov, Oded, & Mann, Devin M. (2021). Telemedicine and healthcare disparities: A cohort study in a large healthcare system in New York City during COVID-19. *Journal of the American Medical Informatics Association, 28*(1), 33–41.

Collins, Patricia H. (2019). *Intersectionality as critical social theory.* Duke University Press.

Collins, Patricia H., & Bilge, S. (2016). *Intersectionality.* Cambridge, UK: Polity Press.

Corus, Canan, & Saatcioglu, Bige (2015). An intersectionality framework for transformative services research. *The Service Industries Journal, 35*(7–8), 415–429.

Crenshaw, Kimberlé (1989). Demarginalizing the intersection of race and sex: A black feminist critique of antidiscrimination doctrine, feminist theory and antiracist politics. *University of Chicago Legal Forum, 1989*(1), 139–167.

Crenshaw, Kimberlé (1991). Mapping the margins: Intersectionality, identity politics, and violence against women of color. *Stanford Law Review, 43*(6), 1241–1299.

Dalsania, Ankur K., Fastiggi, Matthew J., Kahlam, Aaron, Shah, Rajvi, Patel, Krishan, Shiau, Stephanie, Rokicki, Slawa, & DallaPiazza, Michelle (2021). The relationship between social determinants of health and racial disparities in COVID-19 mortality. *Journal of Racial and Ethnic Health Disparities, 9*(1), 288–295.

Dennissen, Marjolein, Benschop, Yvonne, & van den Brink, Marieke (2020). Rethinking diversity management: An intersectional analysis of diversity networks. *Organization Studies, 41*(2), 219–240.

Diamond, Lisa C., Jacobs, Elizabeth A., & Karliner, Leah (2020). Providing equitable care to patients with limited dominant language proficiency amid the COVID-19 pandemic. *Patient Education and Counseling, 103*(8), 1451–1452.

Fitzgerald, Elizabeth, & Campinha-Bacote, Josepha (2019). An intersectionality approach to the process of cultural competemility – Part II. *OJIN: The Online Journal of Issues in Nursing, 24*(2).

Gabrielli, Joy, & Lund, Emily (2020). Acute-on-chronic stress in the time of COVID-19: Assessment considerations for vulnerable youth populations. *Pediatric Research, 88*(6), 829–831.

Gopaldas, Ahir (2013). Intersectionality 101. *Journal of Public Policy & Marketing, 32*(Suppl. 1), 90–94.

Guy, Mary E., & Newman, Meredith A. (2004). Women's jobs, men's jobs: Sex segregation and emotional labor. *Public Administration Review, 64*(3), 289–298.

Hankivsky, Olena (2012). Women's health, men's health, and gender and health: Implications of intersectionality. *Social Science & Medicine, 74*(11), 1712–1720.

Hankivsky, Olena (2014). Intersectionality 101. *The Institute for Intersectionality Research & Policy, SFU,* 1–34.

Hankivsky, Olena, & Christoffersen, Ashlee (2008). Intersectionality and the determinants of health: A Canadian perspective. *Critical Public Health, 18*(3), 271–283.

Hassiotis, Angela (2020). The intersectionality of ethnicity/race and intellectual and developmental disabilities: Impact on health profiles, service access and mortality. *Journal of Mental Health Research in Intellectual Disabilities, 13*(3), 171–173.

Henley, Tiffany J., & Boshier, Maureen (2016). The future of Indian health services for native Americans in the United States: An analysis of policy options and recommendations. *Health Economics, Policy and Law, 11*(4), 397–414.

Himmelstein, Mary S., Puhl, Rebecca M., & Quinn, Diane M. (2017). Intersectionality: An understudied framework for addressing weight stigma. *American Journal of Preventive Medicine, 53*(4), 421–431.

Hull, Shawnika, Stevens, Robin, & Cobb, Jasmine (2020). Masks are the new condoms: Health communication, intersectionality and racial equity in COVID-times. *Health Communication, 35*(14), 1740–1742.

Lokot, Michelle, & Avakyan, Yeva (2020). Intersectionality as a lens to the COVID-19 pandemic: Implications for sexual and reproductive health in development and humanitarian contexts. *Sexual and Reproductive Health Matters, 28*(1), 1764748.

López, Nancy, & Gadsden, Vivian L. (2016). Health inequities, social determinants, and intersectionality. *NAM Perspectives, 6*(12).

López, Nancy, Vargas, Edward D., Juarez, Melina, Cacari-Stone, Lisa, & Bettez, Sonia (2018). What's your "street race"? Leveraging multidimensional measures of race and intersectionality for examining physical and mental health status among Latinxs. *Sociology of Race and Ethnicity, 4*(1), 49–66.

Macias Gil, Raul M, Marcelin, Jasmine R., Zuniga-Blanco, Brenda, Marquez, Carina, Mathew, Trini, & Piggott, Damani A. (2020). COVID-19 pandemic: Disparate health impact on the Hispanic/Latinx population in the United States. *The Journal of Infectious Diseases, 222*(10), 1592–1595.

Mackey, Katherine, Ayers, Chelsea K., Kondo, Karli K., Saha, Somnath, Advani, Shailesh M., Young, Sarah, . . . & Kansagara, Devan (2021). Racial and ethnic disparities in COVID-19 – related infections, hospitalizations, and deaths: A systematic review. *Annals of Internal Medicine, 174*(3), 362–373.

Maestripieri, Lara (2021). The Covid-19 pandemics: Why intersectionality matters. *Frontiers in Sociology, 6*, 642662.

Matthewman, Steve, & Huppatz, Kate (2020). A sociology of Covid-19. *Journal of Sociology, 56*(4), 675–683.

McCall, Leslie (2005). The complexity of intersectionality. *Signs: Journal of Women in Culture and Society, 30*(3), 1771–1800.

Montalvo-Liendo, Nora, Page, Robin, Chilton, Jenifer, Nava, Angeles (2021). Nurse-led long-term support groups for Latina women survivors of intimate partner violence. *Journal of Aggression, Conflict, and Peace Research, 14*(1), 3–13.

Nazareno, Jennifer, Yoshioka, Emily, Adia, Alexander C., Restar, Arjee, Operario, Don, & Choy, Catherine C. (2021). From imperialism to inpatient care: Work differences of Filipino and White registered nurses in the United States and implications for COVID-19 through an intersectional lens. *Gender, Work & Organization, 28*(4), 1426–1446.

Nkomo, Stella, & Hoobler, Jenny M. (2014). A historical perspective on diversity ideologies in the United States: Reflections on human resource management research and practice. *Human Resource Management Review, 24*(3), 245–257.

Obinna, Denise N. (2021). Essential and undervalued: Health disparities of African American women in the COVID-19 era. *Ethnicity & Health, 26*(1), 68–79.

Orgera, Kenal, Garfield, Rachel, & Rudowitz, Robin (2021). *Implications of COVID-19 for social determinants of health.* Kaiser Family Foundation. Retrieved from www.kff.org/coronavirus-covid-19/issue-brief/implications-of-covid-19-for-social-deter minants-of-health/

Prasad, Kriti, McLoughlin, Colleen, Stillman, Martin, Poplau, Sara, Goelz, Elizabeth, Taylor, Sam, . . . & Sinsky, Christine A. (2021). Prevalence and correlates of stress and burnout among US healthcare workers during the COVID-19 pandemic: A national cross-sectional survey study. *EClinicalMedicine, 35,* 100879.

Preti, Emanuele, Di Mattei, Valentina, Perego, Gaia, Ferrari, Federica, Mazzetti, Martina, Taranto, Paola, . . . & Calati, Raffaella (2020). The psychological impact of epidemic and pandemic outbreaks on healthcare workers: Rapid review of the evidence. *Current Psychiatry Reports, 22*(8), 1–22.

Quinn, Katherine G. (2019). Applying an intersectional framework to understand syndemic conditions among young Black gay, bisexual, and other men who have sex with men. *Social Science & Medicine, 295,* 112779.

Razai, Mohammad S., Kankam, Hadyn K., Majeed, Azeem, Esmail, Aneez, & Williams, David R. (2021). Mitigating ethnic disparities in covid-19 and beyond. *BMJ, 372,* 1–5.

Richey, Rebecca, & Pointer, Olivia (2021). Clinical case study of abbreviated cognitive behavioral therapy through an intersectional lens for women health-care workers during the era of COVID-19. *Psychotherapy, 59*(2), 234–244.

Rozenfeld, Yelena, Beam, Jennifer, Maier, Haley, Haggerson, Whitney, Boudreau, Karen, Carlson, Jamie, & Medows, Rhonda (2020). A model of disparities: Risk factors associated with COVID-19 infection. *International Journal for Equity in Health, 19*(1), 1–10.

Ryan, Nessa E., & El Ayadi, Alison M. (2020). A call for a gender-responsive, intersectional approach to address COVID-19. *Global Public Health, 15*(9), 1404–1412.

Samra, Rajvinder, & Hankivsky, Olena (2021). Adopting an intersectionality framework to address power and equity in medicine. *The Lancet, 397*(10277), 857–859.

Satterwhite, Frank J. O., Fernandopulle, Anushka, and Teng, Shiree (2007). Culturally-based capacity building: An approach to working in communities of color for social change. In *Organizational development and capacity in cultural competence.* San Francisco, CA: CompassPoint Nonprofit Services and Los Angeles, CA: The California Endowment. Retrieved May 21, 2008, from www.compasspoint.org/assets/496_satterwhitefull.pdf

Sekalala, Sharifah, Perehudoff, Katrina, Parker, Michael, Forman, Lisa, Rawson, Belinda, & Smith, Maxwell (2021). An intersectional human rights approach to prioritising access to COVID-19 vaccines. *BMJ Global Health,* 6(2), e004462.

Shaffner, Ellen C., Mills, Albert J., & Mills, Jean H. (2019). Intersectional history: Exploring intersectionality over time. *Journal of Management History, 25*(4), 444–463.

Sivashanker, Karthik, Couillard, Cheri, Goldsmith, Jennifer, Walker, Normella, & Eappen, Sunil (2020). Addressing the caste system in US healthcare in the era of COVID-19. *International Journal for Equity in Health, 19*(1), 1–4.

Van Herk, Kimberley A., Smith, Dawn, & Andrew, Caroline (2011). Examining our privileges and oppressions: Incorporating an intersectionality paradigm into nursing. *Nursing Inquiry, 18*(1), 29–39.

Viruell-Fuentes, Edna A., Miranda, Patricia Y., & Abdulrahim, Sawsan (2012). More than culture: Structural racism, intersectionality theory, and immigrant health. *Social Science & Medicine, 75*(12), 2099–2106.

Vizheh, Maryam, Qorbani, Mostafa, Arzaghi, Seyed M., Muhidin, Salut, Javanmard, Zohreh, & Esmaeili, Marzieh (2020). The mental health of healthcare workers in the COVID-19 pandemic: A systematic review. *Journal of Diabetes & Metabolic Disorders, 19*(2), 1967–1978.

Walker, Tahirah J., & Muñoz Rojas, Lizette A. (2021). Teaching and gaining a voice: A rhetorical intersectionality approach to pedagogy of feminist organizational communication. *Management Communication Quarterly, 35*(1), 17–42.

Weber, Lynn, & Parra-Medina, Deborah (2003). Intersectionality and women's health: Charting a path to eliminating health disparities. In M. Texler Segal, V. Demos, & J. J. Kronenfeld (Eds.), *Gender perspectives on health and medicine* (Vol. 7, pp. 181–230). Bingley, England: Emerald Group Publishing Limited.

Wesp, Linda M., Malcoe, Lorraine H., Elliott, Ayana, & Poteat, Tonia (2019). Intersectionality research for transgender health justice: A theory-driven conceptual framework for structural analysis of transgender health inequities. *Transgender Health, 4*(1), 287–296.

Wilson, Will, Bangs, Angela, & Hatting, Tammy (2015). The future of rural behavioral health. *National Rural Health Association Policy Brief.* Retrieved from: The-Future-of-Rural-Behavioral-Health_Feb-2015.pdf

Wilson, Yolonda, White, Amina, Jefferson, Akilah, & Danis, Marion (2019). Intersectionality in clinical medicine: The need for a conceptual framework. *The American Journal of Bioethics, 19*(2), 8–19.

Women's Nonprofit Leadership Initiative. (2022). *The gender gap in nonprofit boardrooms. The 2019 census of women board members of the 50 largest medical and educational institutions in greater Philadelphia.* Retrieved from https://wnli.org/studies/#2019

Young, Ruth, Ayiasi, Richard M., Shung-King, Maylene, & Morgan, Rosemary (2021). Health systems of oppression: Applying intersectionality in health systems to expose hidden inequities. *Health Policy and Planning, 35*(9), 1228–1230.

Zanoni, Patrizia, Janssens, Maddy, Benschop, Yvonne, & Nkomo, Stella (2010). Guest editorial: Unpacking diversity, grasping inequality: Rethinking difference through critical perspectives. *Organization, 17*(1), 9–29.

Zeinali, Zahra, Muraya, Kui, Molyneux, Sassy, & Morgan, Rosemary (2021). The use of intersectional analysis in assessing women's leadership progress in the health workforce in LMICs: A review. *International Journal of Health Policy and Management,* 1–12.

4 Women Falling Through the Cracks

Intersectionality During Crisis and Implications for Human Resource Management

Thanh Thi Hoang, Ravin R. Cline, and Meghna Sabharwal

Introduction

In every organization, human resource management (HRM) is a core function, assuring the right people are recruited, retained, trained, and compensated (Ingraham & Rubaii-Barrett, 2007), while also achieving effective performance outcomes through strategic HRM processes and policies (Boselie, Dietz, & Boon, 2005). Yet, understanding the impact of crisis on HRM remains understudied (Ererdi, Nurgabdeshov, Kozhakhmet, Rofcanin, & Demirbag, 2022).

The world's economic stability was shaken by the outbreak of the COVID-19 virus. By June 2021, the pandemic had infected more than 30,000,000 Americans and taken nearly 600,000 lives (CDC, 2021), with more than 6 million deaths around the world (WHO, 2022). Consequently, the COVID-19 crisis required HR professionals and leaders to go beyond traditional tasks to address complexities they never anticipated (Chang, Chin, & Lee, 2022).

The COVID-19 pandemic exposed how women, Black, and Hispanic workers were disproportionately represented among frontline and essential workers, and experienced unequal impact due to systemic racism, inequities, and discrimination in the workplace (Fairlie, Couch, & Xu, 2020; Landivar, Ruppanner, Scarborough, & Collins, 2020; Shah, Sachdeva, & Dodiuk-Gad, 2020; Vyas, 2022; Yavorsky, Qian, & Sargent, 2021). In the face of a global pandemic, the fight to expand workplace diversity, equity, and inclusion (DEI) is more essential than ever and underscores the need for HRM to safeguard and foster these values.

The pandemic further pushed vulnerable populations, including many essential and front-line workers, women, and racial groups, to the fringes, and they now stand at a greater risk of falling through the cracks in

DOI: 10.4324/9781003184621-4

comparison to pre-pandemic times (Fairlie et al., 2020). The narrowing of the gender wage gap during the pandemic is less a sign of progress than a reminder that the majority of jobs lost were by women working in lower-paying jobs and in the lower socioeconomic strata of society (Institute for Women's Policy Research, 2021). Workers are marginalized by intersections of their gender, sexuality, race, and class (McBride, Hebson, & Holgate, 2015), and in the wake of the COVID-19 crisis, HRM has been called upon to manage through an intersectional lens (Bowleg, 2020; Ryan & Briggs, 2019; Ryan & El Ayadi, 2020).

This chapter examines women in the workforce through the intersections of gender, race, socioeconomic status, sector, and level of analysis. It also responds to the existing literature gap and illustrates how these intersectionalities contribute to disproportionate impacts for women. We argue that an intersectional approach is critical for HRM professionals and organizations to understand deep-rooted inequalities and oppression facing women in the workforce and for the HRM field to redefine its goals and means.

COVID-19 Amplifies Intersectional HRM Challenges

As we head into a *"new normal"* of post-pandemic work, HRM is poised to rethink how intersectionality affects workplace work-life policies, particularly for marginalized employees. Kimberlé Crenshaw (1989) coined the term "intersectionality" to explain that diversity and its dimensions, such as gender, race, sexuality, and class, are inseparable in shaping individual experiences. She argued that no single category could fully explain the cause, as well as the operation, of inequality and oppression. Social categories such as gender, race, class, and economic status exist in entangled relationships that require an intersectional approach to understanding inequity. Intersectionality is essential to understanding how oppression and power structures lead to inequity in the workplace, and it is critical for designing new approaches for inclusive HRM practices that consider gender, race, ethnicity, caregiving responsibilities, socioeconomic status, and sexual orientation (Cho, Crenshaw, & McCall, 2013; Bowleg, 2020; Ryan & Briggs, 2019; Ryan & El Ayadi, 2020). It is common to find HRM policies, programs, and resources developed for majority groups being applied to minoritized groups. For example, general leadership programs for male workers are repurposed for Black, Hispanic, or Latina women without careful consideration of the unique and intersectional identities and experiences of these groups. Women face more obstacles than men in attaining higher leadership positions due to long-established inequality and implicit bias (Sabharwal, 2015). Discriminatory experiences of Black women are vastly different from those of White women, while single women and mothers with children confront different barriers. To develop effective policies that redress discriminatory practices, one must first understand these intersectional relationships (Crenshaw, 1989). Failing to account for intersectionality will undermine even well-intentioned workplace HRM DEI policies.

Framing Intersectional Levels of Analysis

Examinations of intersectional social categories must also include recognition of macro, micro, and meso levels of analysis. Intersectional lenses invite us to question the ways disparities and inequalities manifest themselves from the societal level to organizational practices and individuals (see Figure 4.1). This also suggests that solutions need to acknowledge and embrace all levels. The macro level focuses on global and national societal frameworks for HRM. The meso level addresses the organizational focus for HRM. At the micro level, the focus moves to individuals and groups within organizations (Mor Barak, 2000). For instance, HRM practices (macro) that foster understanding and incorporation of the intersectional needs of employees (micro) is essential to fostering an inclusive and welcoming workplace environment within organizations (meso), which in turn contribute to a cultural norm of inclusion within society as a whole (macro). Not only must gender and race be considered, but other dimensions of diversity that are traditionally

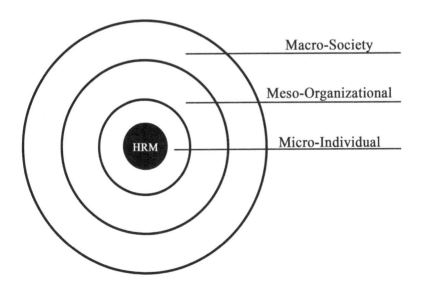

Figure 4.1 Macro/Meso/Micro Levels of Analysis

ignored, such as (dis)ability, religion, sexuality, and socioeconomic status must be considered, in order to support individual employee success.

At the macro level, the intersectional approach suggests that oppressions and inequalities suffered by women are deeply rooted in economic, political, and social structures and beliefs. Global and national cultures play critical roles in shaping organizational norms, determining how employees are treated and evaluated. Inequalities and oppression experienced at the individual micro level reflect multiple systems of privilege and oppression at the macro and meso levels.

At the meso level, crisis often disrupts organizational norms, practices, and cultures. Leading and managing workforces is challenging at the best of times, and workplace policies must be flexible and nimble to adjust to unexpected and sudden changes in needs exposed by crisis. As a result of the COVID-19 pandemic, HR professionals are confronting the complexity of new expectations for workplaces as well as numerous other vexing issues that have been exposed, many of which will be discussed in the next sections. An intersectional meso approach invites HR professionals to pay more attention to the combined effects of gender, race, class, and other identities on HRM organizational practices. HR professionals must question pre-existing assumptions and biases that can impede marginalized groups from receiving equal treatment.

At the micro level, HR attention to the individual needs of employees is perhaps even more urgent in terms of physical and emotional well-being of the individuals rather than a more traditional HR focus on recruitment, retention, productivity, etc. During these tough times, HR professionals worked to focus on employees' general welfare and safety. For instance, the ongoing COVID-19 crisis has seen higher levels of stress, anxiety, and feelings of isolation (Sriharan et al., 2020) for workers, raising alarms at both the meso and macro levels.

The macro/meso/micro levels of analysis also overlap, or intersect, with social categories such as gender, race, socioeconomic status, as well as sectors within the workforce. In the following sections we will discuss each of these intersectional categories and weave in discussion of the macro/meso/micro levels. In Figure 4.2, we present the intersectional "lenses" of gender, race, sector, socioeconomic status discussed within this chapter as well as recognition of the vast array of other overlapping intersectional identities grounded in social, cultural, and organizational (to name just a few) groups. These influence all aspects of human experiences that we use within this chapter to examine inherent inequalities and oppression confronting women in the workplace. We invite HRM professionals to reconsider traditional practices that undermine equal and inclusive efforts, framed within the context of crisis.

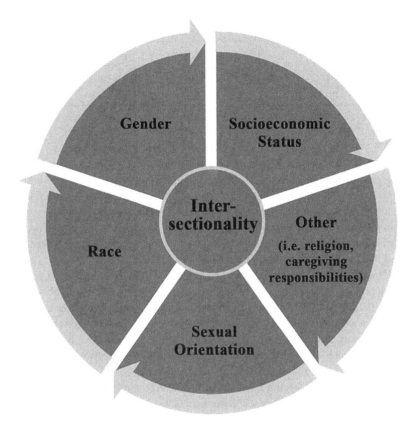

Figure 4.2 Intersectionality of Identities

Gender and the "She-cession"

Women represent nearly half of the U.S. working population and are major drivers of the US economy. In 2019, 76,852 million women aged 16 and above represented 47% of the workforce (U.S. Bureau of Labor Statistics, 2022). Historically, women in the labor force have been subject to persistent wage gaps in all occupations and unequal workplace treatment (U.S. Department of Labor, 2019). In 1979, women earned only 62 cents for every dollar men made (U.S. Bureau of Labor Statistics, 2022). Women made progress by 2020, but, as Table 4.1 indicates, still earned only 82 cents to the dollar men earned. Moreover, women make up a majority of low-paying jobs such as food service, housekeeping, and personal care (Patrick, Berlan, &

Table 4.1 Women's Earnings as Percentages of Men's from 1979 to 2020

Year	Earning %	Year	Earning %	Year	Earning %
1979	62.3	1995	75.5	2010	81.2
1980	64.2	2000	76.9	2015	81.1
1985	68.1	2005	81.0	2020	82.3
1990	71.9				

Source: Adapted from U.S. Bureau of Labor Statistics, 2022

Harwood, 2018). Indeed, women comprise two-thirds of the 40 lowest pay-ing jobs in the U.S. (under $11.50/hour) (Patrick et al., 2018). Even more discouraging, women of color, including Black or African American, His-panic or Latina, and Native Americans experience even larger wage gaps due to the structural inequalities caused by the intersection of gender, race, class, and ethnicity. These patterns are likely to persist, preventing women and their families from attaining wealth (Patrick et al., 2018).

The COVID-19 pandemic disproportionately affected women's employ-ment and income, where, unlike previous crises, women lost more jobs than men. In fact, women lost more than 5.4 million jobs, which translates to 55% of the overall net pandemic job loss (Ewing-Nelson, 2021) largely because of their employment in hard hit industries such as food service, hospitality, and healthcare sectors where BIPOC women are disproportionately repre-sented (Boesch & Phadke, 2021). Women accounted for 91.1% of lost jobs in the public sector, giving rise to what is now commonly known as a "She-cession" (Fabrizio, Gomes, & Tavares, 2021). In most instances during this period, women's earnings and family financial security were reduced irreversibly. For low-income families where women are more likely to be breadwinners, the impact of decreased earnings was more severe. Given that women's poverty rate has always surpassed men's, the disproportion-ate job losses for those who are also disproportionately represented in the lowest income industries, illustrate the overwhelming, and intersectional, impacts of crisis (Semega, Kollar, Shrider, & Creamer, 2020).

Part of the dynamics of the "she-cession" was the impact of family care responsibilities on women's employment status. Though gender norms are changing, women continue to carry a greater proportion of unpaid caregiv-ing work, affecting their workplace contributions and productivity, all of which were magnified by COVID-19. During the pandemic, long-standing gender inequalities intensified work-family conflict and forced many women to reduce their working hours or choose low-wage jobs as an eco-nomic trade-off (Collins, Landivar, Ruppanner, & Scarborough, 2021; Rhu-bart, 2020). Women with young children are more likely to be engaged in unpaid household labor that resulted in reduced hours of paid employment, with no similar impacts for fathers (Glynn, 2018). For married women of color, additional challenges persist, including the lack of flexible work-place policies, unpaid leave, unaffordable childcare, and implicit workplace discrimination. Marital status further frames the experiences of women of color and inequality. Poverty rates for families led by unmarried mothers were high: 35% of Black families, 34% of Hispanic or LatinX families, and 43% of Native American families lived in poverty (Fins, 2020).

On the meso and macro levels, there have been minimal policies established to create equitable, family-friendly, and supportive work environments, which negatively affects performance and advancement, disproportionately impacting women across all intersectional dimensions. Even before the pandemic, only 20% of employees participating in childcare programs were satisfied (U.S. Department of Commerce, 2019). During and after the pandemic, many women were forced to leave the labor force, unable to find or afford childcare following the closure of childcare and school facilities, or due to educational responsibilities for young children necessitated by shifts to remote learning. According to Elias and D'Agostino (2021), women in general, communities of lower-income, and communities of color, carried a disparate amount of childcare responsibility during COVID-19; and since childcare facilities already abide by strict guidelines, the intensification of these standards led many childcare facilities to close. The partial reopening of schools and daycare facilities did little to ameliorate the stress of women with children. Telecommuting was not a gender-neutral benefit. Mothers who telecommute spent much more time than fathers doing housework. In households where both parents work, mothers also provided about 60% of childcare needs (Karageorge, 2020).

Organizations have the power to help women from all groups to be more effective border-crossers so that they can attend to both work and home needs (Barhate & Hirudayaraj, 2021). Policies that provide more time and flexibility to attend to family responsibilities should not be equated with the organization's loss of time, money, and labor. Instead, they should be seen as investments that improve employee motivation, engagement, and retention. HR professionals should consider creating a balanced family-friendly work environment that supports employees across the gender spectrum to fulfill their family and work responsibilities, including paid parental leave and childcare assistance. HRM structures and policies serve as pivotal links between organizational (meso) and individual (micro) levels, particularly during crisis. Leadership and direct supervisor support are critical elements of organizational crisis management, alleviating stress and adjusting employee work-life expectations on an individual basis (Kaur & Shah, 2021; Kossek, Pichler, Bodner, & Hammer, 2011).

Race and Socioeconomic Status: New Crisis, Old Realities

Women of color have historically been subjected to unfair treatment and implicit bias at work. They consistently fall behind in every measurement of income, earnings, and wealth. As the COVID-19 pandemic was wreaking havoc globally, multiple intersections made women more vulnerable to unemployment and poverty. The COVID-19 pandemic illustrates that the one-size-fits-all/women as a monolith group approach is insufficient to address the challenges resulting from intersectionality, especially for vulnerable groups.

Women of color comprise more than 20% of the total workforce. Among all employed women workers in 2019, 16.2% were identified as Hispanic or Latina, 13.8% as Black or African American, and 6.5% as Asian (U.S. Bureau of Labor Statistics, 2022). Alarmingly, women of color fall behind White women in wealth and earnings as they disproportionately work in low-wage industries and are more susceptible to income inequality, poverty, and unemployment. The top five occupations held by women of color in the US are cashiers, housekeeping, registered nurses, customer service representatives, and nursing assistants (Frye, 2020). This results in persistently high poverty rates among Black (18%), Hispanic or Latina (15%), and Native American women (18%) (Fins, 2020). Inadequate attention is given to eliminating race-based disparities. For every dollar that White, non-Hispanic men earned in 2019, Hispanic or Latina women earned only 55 cents, and Black American women earned 65 cents. Clearly, considering women of color as a monolith racial group without recognizing differences in each subgroup is insufficient to develop holistic solutions. For example, Nepalese, Fijian, and Cambodian women made only around 50 cents (Tucker, 2021).

The COVID-19 pandemic continued to push women of color into an unbreakable chain of poverty and inequality. Figure 4.3 illustrates the disproportionate impact of job loss on women, and particularly women of color, during COVID-19. In 2020, the unemployment rate of women was higher than men. This pattern intensified during the COVID-19 pandemic. Table 4.2 compares the unemployment rate across races and genders during two crises: the 2008 Economic Downturn and the 2020 COVID-19 pandemic. The unemployment rate for women of color was consistently higher than White women, with the disparities even more pronounced during the pandemic. Many jobs deemed "essential," such as healthcare and food service, are dominated by women and women of color. These jobs were not impacted as severely during the pandemic, thereby implying that job losses for women in other employment categories were even more startling.

Women of color may not have the luxury of choosing to work from home. White male and female workers are more likely in middle and senior leadership positions, allowing them to telecommute and work remotely.

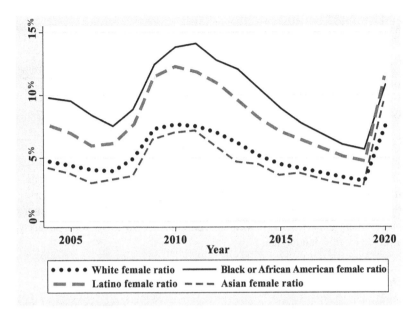

Figure 4.3 Women's Unemployment Rate by Race from 2004 to 2020

Source: Adapted U.S. Bureau of Labor Statistics (2022)

In contrast, women of color are strikingly absent from these positions (Beckwith, Carter, & Peters, 2016; Bloch, Taylor, Church, & Buck, 2020; Sanchez-Hucles & Davis, 2010) and are highly concentrated in front-line, low-wage jobs where they are subject to lay-offs, furloughs, and unpaid leave (Thomas et al., 2020), with few options to work remotely. Women of color are also less likely to be protected and supported by policies that allow for affordable childcare and paid family leave. As such, it will likely be more challenging for women of color to rebound from the pandemic than for White women (Thomas et al., 2020).

Sectoral Lens: Inequivalent Challenges

The COVID-19 pandemic resulted in unprecedented implications across industry sectors. Thousands of businesses, nonprofits, and public organizations experienced interruption, closure, and labor shortages. As presented previously, this has resulted in unequal challenges for women, women of color, and women in lower socioeconomic categories compared with men. Intersectional framing suggests that social components such as economy

Table 4.2 Comparison of Unemployment Rate (%) During Two Crises by Race and Gender

Race	2020		2008	
	Men	Women	Men	Women
White	7.0	7.6	5.5	4.9
Black/African American	12.1	10.9	11.4	8.9
Hispanic/Latino ethnicity	9.7	11.4	4.1	3.7
Asian	7.8	9.6	7.6	7.7

Source: Adapted from U.S. Bureau of Labor Statistics, 2022

and sectoral structure are closely related to how women experience inequalities and disadvantages. Understanding this impact across sectors during the COVID-19 crisis offers a clear example. In this section, we explore inequivalent experiences of women working in sectors that were severely affected by this pandemic.

Healthcare and Hospitality

Healthcare and hospitality are among the industries hit hardest by COVID-19 (see Silverio, Montalvo-Liendo, & Carrizales, 2023), raising an alarm for HRM. In the healthcare industry, 70% of health workers are women and 40% are people of color (Sánchez, Vale, Rodrigues, & Surita, 2020), making them the first targets of the COVID-19 virus. Over 898,000 infected cases and 2,240 deaths by June 2022 were among healthcare staff (CDC, 2021). Female healthcare workers experienced an immense amount of stress, depression, and burnout during the pandemic due to numerous individual, organizational, and systemic factors (Sriharan et al., 2020). In the hospitality industry, women make up more than half (51%) of the workforce (Fins, 2020). Women accounted for the majority of job losses (54%) in this sector in the first two months of the virus outbreak. Even when the job market improved, women employed in hospitality worked fewer hours and struggled to make ends meet. Many were forced to risk their families' safety (through exposure in the workplace) working in jobs that were largely underpaid. The poverty rate for employees working in the hospitality industry is consistently higher for Black or African American, Hispanic or Latina women, and women born outside the US.

STEMM Industry and Academia

Women are missing opportunities for social mobility as they account for only 28% of the workforce in Science, Technology, Engineering, Math, and Medicine (STEMM), the industry that is associated with higher earning jobs (Trapani & Hale, 2019). In academia, women account for a larger population, yet, they fall behind men regarding publications, tenure track positions, and leadership positions (Harmon, Hopkins, Kelchen, Persky, & Roy, 2018; Knepper, Scutelnicu, & Tekula, 2020). Women of color are particularly underrepresented in both. Gender and racial gaps have been long-standing issues and remain difficult to rectify due to numerous factors, including gender stereotypes, male-dominated culture, and implicit bias in the workplace (Hill, Corbett, & St. Rose, 2010).

COVID-19 exacerbated HRM's ability to maintain a productive and inclusive workforce. In general women face more layoffs than men in STEMM fields, and this continued during the pandemic (NASEM, 2021). Moreover, STEMM growth and promotion opportunities are not equally distributed to women. Women in STEMM leadership positions are more likely to work in less prestigious institutions with access to fewer resources, and their progress in academe, normally fragile, worsened during COVID-19 (NASEM, 2021). During COVID-19, many women could not successfully work from home due to family and unpaid responsibilities, adversely affecting their scholarly productivity. In fact, women published fewer papers and were cited less than men during the crisis outbreak, which can affect their career trajectory and professional growth leadership opportunities (Cui, Ding, & Zhu, 2022; Krukowski, Montoya Williams, & Cardel, 2022). Moreover, COVID-19 disrupted academic schedules and increased workload resulting in mental health risks for women (NASEM, 2021).

Nonprofit Sector

Over 1.5 million nonprofit jobs were lost due to COVID-19, about 7.4% of the nonprofit workforce (Rendon, 2021). With women accounting for nearly 75% of the nonprofit workforce (Miller & Vagins, 2018), most job losses fell on female employees (Rendon, 2021). Nonprofits were forced to deal with urgent, often catastrophic, shifts in service demands at the same time that revenue sources were severely diminished (Kuenzi, Stewart, & Walk, 2021). As many nonprofits work closely with the community to provide essential services (see Diggs, Castillo-Krewson, & McCandless, 2023), social distancing protocols meant organizations had to cancel, postpone, or modify activities for an unknown period. In the art and culture subsector, part-time employees and artists experienced difficult times finding jobs due to the cancellation of performances and shows. In subsectors such as human services, education, and healthcare, nonprofits did not have enough employees and volunteers to keep up with surging demands for help. Moreover, many low-paying jobs typically held by women, like teaching assistants, direct social services, or food services are not amenable to remote work (Evans & Knepper, 2022; Rendon, 2021), putting many women in these jobs at higher risk of contracting the COVID-19 virus. Losing female volunteers is another obstacle for nonprofit leaders, especially when this sector relies on the voluntary workforce, with many women unable to volunteer due to stay-at-home orders, health concerns, family care responsibilities, and transportation issues, among others. Historically, volunteering has been female-focused, with women volunteers outnumbering men and women volunteering more hours (AmeriCorps, 2021). However, volunteering is a privileged activity, linked to many of the same challenges and barriers discussed in the HR realm (Neely, Lengnick-Hall, & Evans, 2022).

The impact of COVID-19 on nonprofits was also uneven across racial and ethnic categories. Nonprofits led by Black leaders disproportionately experienced employee layoffs: 43.5% of Black-led nonprofit organizations laid off employees compared to 20.7% of Hispanic or Latino-led nonprofits and 28.1% of any People of Color (POC) led nonprofits (Texas Nonprofit Leaders, 2020). These HR challenges bleed into the organization's ability to maintain programs and meet the intensifying needs of the clients.

HRM in a New Normal

COVID-19 altered the way we work and perceive work. HRM systems across sectors experienced workplace changes at a speed and scale that had never been experienced before. Many organizations were forced to reinvent and change their ways of working and managing. However, these changes need to be accompanied by a revisiting of traditional assumptions and structures of HRM systems, from performance and productivity evaluation to job design and benefits.

In transitioning to a new normal, HRM professionals struggle to find the best approach to ensure a motivated, productive, and equitable workforce. In April 2020, 62% of employed Americans worked from home compared to 25% prior to the pandemic (Boland, De Smet, Palter, & Sanghvi, 2020). Recent studies of the COVID-19 pandemic present contradictory findings and perceptions for these new approaches, particularly in regards to the cost-effectiveness and productivity in hybrid and telecommuting work environments (Lund et al., 2021; PwC, 2021). On the other hand, as discussed earlier, there are growing concerns about the disproportional effects of the new normal on women and other disadvantaged employee groups. For example, women of color and women working in low-paying jobs have fewer opportunities to choose jobs that give them the flexibility to telecommute. Despite gains, the general HRM framework is not yet equitable and inclusive. Missing are flexible policies to address working mothers' needs for childcare and family care, an issue highlighted by the pandemic. Existing HR policies have long neglected accessible, affordable childcare concerns. Childcare costs are beyond affordability for many families (Bateman & Ross, 2020). These costs have a corresponding impact on women remaining in the workforce. Current HRM policies do not remedy outdated measures of productivity or the unequal burdens placed on women's shoulders, resulting in both intellectual and social capital losses. Even when women choose flexible work, this can be a double-edged sword because part-time, flexible jobs usually offer lower salaries and less comprehensive health insurance.

Performance appraisal based on physical presence in the office, which has been disadvantageous for mothers who choose to telecommute, is becoming obsolete. This can't happen soon enough for women working from home who have long worried their work performance will be negatively judged, based upon impressions of telecommuting or flexible work arrangements as special favors or privileges granted inconsistently (Minbaeva, 2021). One in four pregnant women and new mothers experience unfair treatment at the workplace such as furloughs and are questioned by employers about their commitment (TUC, 2020). Mothers are 2.1 times more likely than fathers to worry about their job performance being judged negatively due to caregiving responsibilities (Thomas et al., 2020). A dangerous stigma is that employers associate all women with childcare responsibilities and discourage women's participation in management opportunities. During the pandemic, these, and other false perceptions about women and working mothers intensified.

Women experience lower job satisfaction, higher levels of anxiety, depression, and burnout (Feng & Savani, 2020; Thomas et al., 2020). Since productivity is the primary measure of value and success, productivity loss sets back gender parity. Work-family conflict, potential productivity reduction, stigmatization of hybrid or telecommuting, emotional and mental strain consequently hinder women from career advancement.

Telecommuting and Digital Access – An Equalizer for Women?

Organizations have come to increasingly rely on modern infrastructure and communication technologies, and the trend will likely persist post-pandemic. One can postulate that the new normal will be an equalizer for all groups of women as they provide more flexibility to pursue careers while attending to family responsibilities. However, as noted previously, COVID-19 has shown us that remote work arrangements are not necessarily beneficial for all women. Without mindful design, new HRM policies will leave women behind and reinforce systemic barriers that prevent women's upward mobility. HRM professionals need to take advantage of lessons learned during COVID-19, to move away from one-size-fits-all policies and instead restructure policies to avoid reinforcing stereotypes or perpetuating inequality. These opportunities include reimagining evaluation and oversight practices, networking and training opportunities, communication structures, and establishing organizational cultures that empathize and support worker needs, regardless of in-person, hybrid, or remote environments (Barhate & Hirudayaraj, 2021).

Included within these efforts, HRM must consider the racial, ethnic, and gender digital gap that significantly widened during the pandemic. According to USAID (2021), women are 14% less likely than men to own a mobile phone, and 43% less likely to engage online worldwide. As digital and information technologies dominate many industries, women are missing out on opportunities to access job information, learn, work, and build their networks (Acilar & Sæbø, 2021). An intersectional lens reveals ownership inequality in internet access, home broadband, and computers, all critical for modern work and study, across different groups. Lower income is associated with a reduced level of technology adoption (Vogels, 2021). Only 57% of low-income Americans have home broadband, compared to 83% of middle-income individuals and 93% of high-income individuals. Low-income adults are also less likely to have smartphones or computers at home (Atske & Perrin, 2021). Further, 29% of Black and 35% of Hispanic or Latino adults did not have a broadband connection (Atske & Perrin, 2021). In addition, 46% of low-income home broadband users worried about their ability to pay for this service (McClain, Vogels, Perrin, Sechopoulos, & Rainie, 2020). The digital divide deprives women and citizens from low income and/or minority backgrounds of education, work, healthcare, and financial stability.

In the transition to remote work, HR professionals are confronting obstacles in managing performance and engaging employees. The post-pandemic workplace will likely see fewer women in physical organization spaces because women have a higher need to work remotely (Killham & Wells, 2021). With more women working from home, and men disproportionately present in the office, women's contributions can be "out of sight, out of mind." HR managers may have a difficult time evaluating their productivity and performance. Remote workers, in many cases women and working mothers, receive less recognition and are less likely to get promoted as compared to employees who are present full-time at work. In fact, women who work remotely were 27% less likely to receive promotions than working men (Killham & Wells, 2021). Platforms for women to assert their power and influence can shrink because of the virtual workspace (Barhate &

Hirudayaraj, 2021). As more women work remotely, they can be left out of informal decision-making spaces that are traditionally male-dominated. In addition, remote employees are more susceptible to bias and discrimination because this work format is associated with lower productivity and engagement. Working remotely won't be an equalizer for women, and especially not for those who are also parents, if it heightens pre-existing bias in performance evaluation and accelerates inherent inequalities.

Rethinking HRM Policies and Approaches

In the previous sections, we applied an intersectional lens to present recurring challenges that women have faced before and during the COVID-19 pandemic, such as persistent pay gap, unemployment, and work/family conflicts. We also discussed issues such as reduced productivity, digital divide, and negative performance judgment when organizations alter their work fashion. Women of color, working mothers, and frontline female employees are shouldering more burdens due to the intersection of their marginalized identities. Women leaving the workforce will undermine DEI efforts and negatively affect thousands of public and private organizations. It is urgent that we reconsider current HRM approaches and champion a paradigm shift toward women with intersectional identities.

Given the changing landscape of the US workforce, what approaches will help organizations effectively protect their employees, address new challenges, and maintain an inclusive and motivated workforce? At the 2021 American Society for Public Administration (ASPA) conference, keynote speaker, Lisa Garrett, Director of Personnel for the County of Los Angeles asserted the COVID-19 pandemic is a critical time for HR leaders in the public sector to keep up their five "superpowers": enhancing and embracing new technology, approaching with empathy, protecting employees' mental wellness, focusing on cross-training and reskilling staffs, and embracing flexibility. Along the same vein, Minbaeva (2021) suggests that the future of work will be influenced by critical megatrends: flexible workforce, digitization of the business model, Artificial Intelligence (AI), and machine learning. These trends provide opportunities for using intersectional analysis to assess why macro level policies such as Equal Employment Opportunity or Nondiscrimination/Anti-Harassment are not fully effective in helping different groups of women in the workforce, especially during crisis. In turn, improving upon these macro level policies will enable HR professionals and leaders to deliver meso level policies for organizations affected by the global and local landscapes. We argue that taking an intersectional perspective is essential for HRM professionals and organizations to deploy these superpowers and adjust to megatrends.

HRM policies that take a holistic, empathetic approach that incorporates intersectional understanding on a micro, meso, and even macro level will address the short-term needs of their employees during and post crisis as well as having long-term implications. Communication in organizations is improved when employees feel their supervisors are empathetic, understanding, and listen (Kwon, Farndale, & Park, 2016). The recent 2021 State of Workplace Empathy Report indicated that a significant portion of the workforce desires empathetic organizational cultures, is more productive and works longer hours, and is even willing to sacrifice lower salaries in exchange for these more empathetic and flexible work environments (Business Solver, 2021). Unfortunately, the same report showed that only a quarter of those employees were satisfied with the current levels of organizational empathy, while at the same time 68% of CEOs worried that showing empathy in the workplace undermined respect for their roles. Empathy is critically important in the changing landscape of the workplace as it creates a psycho-social safe environment where employees feel cared for, understood, and supported. In addition, it helps organizations safeguard diversity and inclusion goals, especially for groups vulnerable to inequalities such as working mothers and women of color.

HRM research has traditionally focused on the idea of permanent organizations and permanent structures while little attention is given to flexible work practices. Current HRM practices are designed based on the assumption that "employment relations are bounded by space, time, and task-based job descriptions, all based on the employer's choices" (Minbaeva, 2021, p. 2). The new normal work structure post-pandemic is drifting away from the traditional "nine-to-five" and "five days per week." Many organizations grapple with the extent to which they should provide employees with flexible schedules, redesigning jobs, managing, and engaging employees across different spaces and times.

Staff mobility occurs not only from one place to another but also across many physical and virtual environments (Collings & Sheeran, 2020). To be proactive and effective, HRM needs to be agile, adapting swiftly to change, while continuing its strategic leadership, championing employees, and serving as technical expert and change consultant (Cayer & Sabharwal, 2013).

Conclusion

The US workforce is structured to favor masculinity whether intentionally or unintentionally. Women and women of color are trapped in low-paying jobs that offer low benefits. Power distance is widened as women are associated with family care and work, while men are expected to assume workplace leadership positions. Crisis, such as the COVID-19 pandemic, is not the root cause of workplace inequalities and disparities. Instead, these disparities are exacerbated in times of crisis through structural racism, sexism, classism, and discrimination.

Intersectionality provides a critical lens to help HR practitioners trace back to the sources of inequality, discrimination, and oppression to identify remedies. The COVID-19 pandemic created a more complex and challenging environment for HR practitioners, reinforcing inherent challenges for women workers. Amid the crisis, thousands of female employees, working mothers, and women of color in many industries lost jobs, struggled to maintain a work-life balance, and to make both ends meet. Health security, job flexibility, and fair performance evaluation were among major concerns identified by women before, during, and post-pandemic. Being tasked with strategic roles to safeguard an equal, diverse, and productive workplace, HR practitioners have the power to protect these critical groups, help them to stay in the workforce, and continue contributing to the economy.

Intersectionality invites us to examine the "why" – why have working mothers and women from low-paid industries been hit harder during the crisis? It lays a foundation for HR practitioners to explore the "how" – how can HRM help these groups participate in the workforce safely, equitably, and productively? To help different groups of women overcome recurring impediments during and after crisis, HR leaders need to rethink existing structures, policies, and culture, rather than returning to traditional workplace norms. This includes how we view work and manage employees, design family-friendly policies, and implement practices to help different groups of women adapt to the new working environment while ensuring their participation, visibility, and upward mobility to leadership positions. While rethinking and redesigning the HRM toolkit is far from an easy task, the global pandemic illustrates that it is critically important to help organizations maintain an equitable and diverse workforce that can successfully adapt to future crises.

References

Acilar, Ali, & Sæbø, Øystein (2021). Towards understanding the gender digital divide: A systematic literature review. *Global Knowledge, Memory and Communication*, (20211216). https://doi.org/10.1108/GKMC-09-2021-0147

AmeriCorps. (2021). *Key findings from the 2019 current population survey: Civic engagement and volunteering supplement*. Retrieved from www.census.gov/newsroom/stories/volunteer-week.html

Atske, Sara, & Perrin, Andrew (2021). *Home broadband adoption, computer ownership vary by race, ethnicity in the U.S.* Retrieved from www.pewresearch.org/facttank/2021/07/16/home-broadband-adoption-computer-ownership-vary-by-raceethnicity-in-the-u-s/

Barhate, Bhagyashree, & Hirudayaraj, Malar (2021). Emerging career realities during the pandemic: What does it mean for women's career development? *Advances in Developing Human Resources*, *23*(3), 253–266.

Bateman, Nicole, & Ross, Martha (2020). Why has COVID-19 been especially harmful for working women. *Brookings.edu.* Retrieved from www.brookings.edu/essay/why-has-covid-19-been-especially-harmful-for-working-women/

Beckwith, A. LaSharnda, Carter, Danon R., & Peters, Tara (2016). The underrepresentation of African American women in executive leadership: What's getting in the way? *Journal of Business Studies Quarterly, 7*(4), 115–134.

Bloch, Katrina R., Taylor, Tiffany, Church, Jacob, & Buck, Alison (2020). An intersectional approach to the glass ceiling: Gender, race and share of middle and senior management in U.S. workplaces. *Sex Roles, 84*(5–6), 312–325.

Boesch, Diana, & Phadke, Shilpa (2021). *When women lose all the jobs: Essential actions for a gender-equitable recovery.* Retrieved from www.americanprogress.org/issues/women/reports/2021/02/01/495209/women-lose-jobs-essential-actionsgender-equitable-recovery/

Boland, Brodie, De Smet, Aaron, Palter, Rob, & Sanghvi, Aditya (2020). *Reimagining the office and work life after COVID-19.* Retrieved from www.mckinsey.com/business-functions/people-and-organizational-performance/our-insights/reimaginingthe-office-and-work-life-after-covid-19

Boselie, Paul, Dietz, Graham, & Boon, Corine (2005). Commonalities and contradictions in HRM and performance research. *Human Resource Management Journal, 15*(3), 67–94.

Bowleg, Lisa (2020). We're not all in this together: On COVID-19, intersectionality, and structural inequality. *American Public Health Association, 110*(7), 917.917.

Business Solver. (2021). *2021 State of workplace empathy: Executive summary.* Retrieved from https://resources.businessolver.com/c/2021-empathy-exec-summ?x=OE03jO

Cayer, N. Joseph, & Sabharwal, Meghna (2013). *Public personnel administration: Managing human capital.* San Diego, CA: Birkdale Publishers.

Centers for Disease Control and Prevention [CDC]. (2021). *Trends in number of COVID-19 cases and deaths in the US reported to CDC, by state/territory.* Retrieved from https://covid.cdc.gov/covid-data-tracker/#trends_dailycases

Chang, Eunmi, Chin, Hyun, & Lee, Jeong W. (2022). Pre-crisis commitment human resource management and employees' attitudes in a global pandemic: The role of trust in the government. *Human Resource Management, 61*(3), 373–387.

Cho, Sumi, Crenshaw, Kimberlé W., & McCall, Leslie (2013). Toward a field of intersectionality studies: Theory, applications, and praxis. *Signs: Journal of Women in Culture and Society, 38*(4), 785–810.

Collings, David G., & Sheeran, Ruthanna (2020). Research insights: Global mobility in a postcovid world. *Irish Journal of Management, 39*(2), 77–84.

Collins, Caitlyn, Landivar, Liana C., Ruppanner, Leah, & Scarborough, William J. (2021). COVID-19 and the gender gap in work hours. *Gender, Work & Organization, 28*(S1), 101–112.

Crenshaw, Kimberlé (1989). Demarginalizing the intersection of race and sex: A Black feminist critique of antidiscrimination doctrine, feminist theory and antiracist politics. *University of Chicago Legal Forum, 1989*(1), 139–167.

Cui, Ruomeng, Ding, Hao, & Zhu, Feng (2022). Gender inequality in research productivity during the COVID-19 pandemic. *Manufacturing & Service Operations Management, 24*(2), 707–726.

Diggs, Schnequa N., Castillo Krewson, Rosa & McCandless, Sean A. (2023). Intersectional disparities during crisis: Improving social equity through public and nonprofit management. In H. J. Knepper, M. D. Evans, & T. J. Henley (Eds.), *Intersectionality & crisis management: A path to social equity*. New York: Routledge.

Elias, Nicole M., & D'Agostino, Maria J. (2021). *Catastrophe and cumulative disadvantage: Laying bare inequity and identifying opportunity*. Paper presented at the American Society for Public Administration (ASPA) 2021 Virtual Conference.

Ererdi, Can, Nurgabdeshov, Assylbek, Kozhakhmet, Sanat, Rofcanin, Yasin, & Demirbag, Mehmet (2022). International HRM in the context of uncertainty and crisis: A systematic review of literature (2000–2018). *International Journal of Human Resource Management, 33*(12), 2503–2540.

Evans, Michelle D., & Knepper, Hillary J. (2022). Gender and nonprofit administration: Past, present and future. In P. Shields & N. M. Elias (Eds.), *Handbook on gender and public administration* (pp. 195–211). Cheltenham, UK and Northampton, MA: Elward Elgar Publishing.

Ewing-Nelson, Claire (2021). All of the jobs lost in December were women's jobs. *National Women's Law Center*. Retrieved from https://nwlc.org/wp-content/uploads/2021/01/December-Jobs-Day.pdf

Fabrizio, Stefania, Gomes, Diego B. P., & Tavares, Marina M. (2021). *COVID-19 She-cession: The employment penalty of taking care of young children*. Retrieved from www. imf.org/en/Publications/WP/Issues/2021/03/03/COVID-19-She-Cession-The-Employment-Penalty-of-Taking-Care-of-Young-Children-50117

Fairlie, Robert W., Couch, Kenneth, & Xu, Huanan (2020). *The impacts of COVID-19 on minority unemployment: First evidence from April 2020 CPS Microdata (No. w27246)*. Retrieved from www.nber.org/papers/w27246

Feng, Zhiyu, & Savani, Krishna (2020). Covid-19 created a gender gap in perceived work productivity and job satisfaction: Implications for dual-career parents working from home. *Gender in Management, 35*(7/8), 719–736.

Fins, Amanda (2020). National snapshot: Poverty among women & families, 2020. *National Women's Law Center*. Retrieved from https://nwlc.org/resource/national-snapshot-poverty-among-women-families-2020/

Frye, Jocelyn (2020). *On the frontlines at work and at home: The disproportionate economic effects of the coronavirus pandemic on women of color*. Center for American Progress. Retrieved from www.americanprogress.org/article/frontlines-workhome/

Glynn, Sarah J. (2018). *An unequal division of labor: How equitable workplace policies would benefit working mothers*. Center for American Progress. Retrieved from www.americanprogress.org/article/unequal-division-labor/

Harmon, Oskar, Hopkins, Barbara, Kelchen, Robert, Persky, Joe, & Roy, Joseph (2018). The annual report on the economic status of the profession, 2017–18. *Academe, 104*(2), 4–10.

Hill, Catherine, Corbett, Christianne, & St. Rose, Andresse (2010). Why so few? Women in science, technology, engineering, and mathematics. *American Association of University Women*. Retrieved from https://eric.ed.gov/?id=ED509653

Ingraham, Patricia W., & Rubaii-Barrett, Nadia (2007). Human resource management as a core dimension of public administration. *Foundations of Public Administration Series*. Retrieved from https://faculty.cbpp.uaa.alaska.edu/afgjp/PADM601%20 Fall%202009/FPA-HRM-Article.pdf

Institute for Women's Policy Research. (2021). *Policy brief: The weekly gender wage gap by race and ethnicity.* Retrieved from https://iwpr.org/wp-content/uploads/2021/03/2021-Weekly-Wage-Gap-Brief-1.pdf

Karageorge, Eleni X. (2020). COVID-19 recession is tougher on women. *Monthly Labor Review*, 1–2.

Kaur, Rajwinder, & Shah, Reena (2021). HR initiatives to establish the new normal in COVID-19 Scenario. *International Management Review, 17*, 40–48.

Killham, Emily, & Wells. Bret (2021). *The gender gap widens: Three critical actions required to support women in the workplace.* Retrieved from https://go.perceptyx.com/gender-gap-widens-support-women-in-the-workplace

Knepper, Hillary J., Scutelnicu, Gina, & Tekula, Rebecca (2020). Why gender and research productivity matters in academia: Exploring evidence from NASPAA-accredited schools. *Journal of Public Affairs Education, 26*(1), 51–72.

Kossek, Ellen E., Pichler, Shaun, Bodner, Todd, & Hammer, Leslie B. (2011). Workplace social support and work – family conflict: A meta-analysis clarifying the influence of general and work – family-specific supervisor and organizational support. *Personnel Psychology, 64*(2), 289–313.

Krukowski, Rebecca A., Montoya Williams, Diana C., & Cardel, Michelle I. (2022). A year into the pandemic: An update on women in science, technology, engineering, math, and medicine. *Annals of the American Thoracic Society, 19*(4), 517–524.

Kuenzi, Kerry, Stewart, Amanda J., & Walk, Marlene (2021). COVID-19 as a nonprofit workplace crisis: Seeking insights from the nonprofit workers' perspective. *Nonprofit Management and Leadership, 31*(4), 821–832.

Kwon, Bora, Farndale, Elaine, & Park, Jong G. (2016). Employee voice and work engagement: Macro, meso, and micro-level drivers of convergence? *Human Resource Management Review, 26*(4), 327–337.

Landivar, Liana C., Ruppanner, Leah, Scarborough, William J., & Collins, Caitlyn (2020). Early signs indicate that COVID-19 is exacerbating gender inequality in the labor force. *Socius: Sociological Research for a Dynamic World, 6*, 1–3.

Lund, Susan, Madgavkar, Anu, Manyika, James, Smit, Sven, Ellingrud, Kweilin, Meaney, Mary, & Robinson, Olivia (2021). *McKinsey global institute: The future of work after COVID-19.* Retrieved from www.mckinsey.com/featured-insights/future-of-work/the-futureof-work-after-covid-19

McBride, Anne, Hebson, Gail, & Holgate, Jane (2015). Intersectionality: Are we taking enough notice in the field of work and employment relations? *Work, Employment and Society, 29*(2), 331–341.

McClain, Colleen, Vogels, Emily A., Perrin, Andrew, Sechopoulos, Stella & Rainie, Lee (2020). *The internet and the pandemic.* Retrieved from www.pewresearch.org/internet/2021/09/01/the-internet-and-the-pandemic/

Miller, Kevin & Vagins, Deborah (2018). Broken ladders: Barriers to women's representation in nonprofit leadership. *American Association of University Women Policy Brief.* Retrieved from www.aauw.org/resources/research/broken-ladders/

Minbaeva, Dana (2021). Disrupted HR? *Human Resource Management Review, 31*(4), 100820.

Mor Barak, Michàl E. (2000). The inclusive workplace: An ecosystems approach to diversity management. *Social work, 45*(4), 339–353.

National Academies of Sciences Engineering Medicine [NASEM]. (2021). *Consensus study report highlights: The impact of COVID-19 on the careers of women in academic science, engineering, and medicine.* Retrieved from www.national academies.org/our-work/investigating-the-potential-impact-of-covid-19-on-the-careers-of-women-in-academic-science-engineering-and-medicine

Neely, Andrea R., Lengnick-Hall, Mark L., & Evans, Michelle D. (2022). A process model of volunteer motivation. *Human Resource Management Review, 32*(4), 100879.

Patrick, Kayla, Berlan, Meika, & Harwood, Morgan (2018, August). Low-wage jobs held primarily by women will grow the most over the next decade. *National Women's Law Center Fact Sheet.* Retrieved from https://nwlc.org/wp-content/uploads/2016/04/Low-Wage-Jobs-Held-Primarily-by-Women-Will-Grow-the-Most-Over-the-Next-Decade-2018.pdf

PwC. (2021). *PwC's US remote work survey.* Retrieved from www.pwc.com/us/en/library/covid-19/us-remote-work-survey.html

Rendon, Jim (2021). Why women don't get ahead: Inequities in nonprofit pay and leadership opportunities are subtle and entrenched. The pandemic could make things worse – or be a chance for real change. *The Chronicle of Philanthropy, 33*(3), 6.

Rhubart, Danielle (2020). Gender disparities in caretaking during the COVID-19 pandemic. *Lerner Center for Public Health Promotion: Population Health Research Brief Series.* Retrieved from https://surface.syr.edu/lerner/54

Ryan, Ann M., & Briggs, Caitlin Q. (2019). Improving work-life policy and practice with an intersectionality lens. *Equality, Diversity and Inclusion: An International Journal, 39*(5), 533–547.

Ryan, Nessa E., & El Ayadi, Alison M. E. (2020). A call for a gender-responsive, intersectional approach to address COVID-19. *Global Public Health, 15*(9), 1404–1412.

Sabharwal, Meghna (2015). From glass ceiling to glass cliff: Women in senior executive service. *Journal of Public Administration Research and Theory, 25*(2), 399–426.

Sánchez, Odette R., Vale, Diama B., Rodrigues, Larissa, & Surita, Fernanda G. (2020). Violence against women during the COVID-19 pandemic: An integrative review. *International Journal of Gynecology & Obstetrics, 151*(2), 180–187.

Sanchez-Hucles, Janis V., & Davis, Donald D. (2010). Women and women of color in leadership: Complexity, identity, and intersectionality. *American Psychologist, 65*(3), 171–181.

Semega, Jessica, Kollar, Melissa, Shrider, Emily, & Creamer, John (2020). *Income and poverty in the United States:2019 (P60–270).* U.S. Census Bureau. Retrieved from www. census.gov/library/publications/2020/demo/p60-270.html

Shah, Monica, Sachdeva, Muskaan, & Dodiuk-Gad, Roni P. (2020). COVID-19 and racial disparities. *Journal of the American Academy of Dermatology, 83*(1), e35.

Silverio, Michelle, Montalvo-Liendo, Nora, & Carrizales, Tony (2023). Intersectionality and healthcare management: The case of crisis and COVID-19. In H. J. Knepper, M. D. Evans, & T. J. Henley (Eds.), *Intersectionality & crisis management: A path to social equity.* New York: Routledge.

Sriharan, Abi, Ratnapalan, Savithiri, Tricco, Andrea, Lupea, Doina, Ayala, Ana P., Pang, Hilary, & Lee, Daniel D. (2020). Occupational stress, burnout, and depression in women in healthcare during COVID-19 pandemic: Rapid scoping review. *Frontiers in Global Women's Health, 1,* 596690.

Texas Nonprofit Leaders. (2020). *COVID-19 impact report.* Retrieved from https://txnonprofits.org/covidimpact/

Thomas, Rachel, Cooper, Marianne, Cardazone, Gina, Urban, Kate, Bohrer, Ali, Long, Madison, . . . Coury, Sarah (2020). *Women in the workplace 2020.* Retrieved from https://wiw-report. s3.amazonaws.com/Women_in_the_Workplace_2020.pdf

Trapani, Josh, & Hale, Katherine (2019). *Higher education in science and engineering. Science & engineering indicators 2020. NSB-2019–7.* National Science Foundation. Retrieved from https://ncses.nsf.gov/pubs/nsb20197/assets/nsb20197.pdf

TUC. (2020). *Pregnant and precarious: new and expectant mums' experiences of work during Covid-19.* Retrieved from www.tuc.org.uk/research-analysis/reports/pregnant-and-precarious-new-and-expectant-mums-experiences-work-during

Tucker, Jasmine (2021). *Asian American and Pacific Islander women lose $10,000 annually to the wage gap.* Retrieved from https://nwlc.org/wp-content/uploads/2020/01/AAPI-EPD-2021-v1.pdf

U.S. Bureau of Labor Statistics. (2022). *Labor force statistics from the current population survey: Demographics.* Retrieved from www.bls.gov/cps/demographics.htm#women

U.S. Department of Commerce. (2019). *Federal employee viewpoint survey results.* Retrieved from www.commerce.gov/sites/default/files/2019-11/Commerce%202019%20FEVS%20Online%20Post.pdf

U.S. Department of Labor. (2019). *Employment and earnings by occupation.* Retrieved from www.dol.gov/agencies/wb/data/occupations

USAID. (2021). *USAID digital strategy 2020–2024.* Retrieved from www.usaid.gov/sites/default/files/documents/USAID_Digital_Strategy.pdf.pdf

Vogels, Emily (2021). *Digital divide persists even as Americans with lower incomes make gains in tech adoption.* Retrieved from www.pewresearch.org/fact-tank/2021/06/22/digital-divide-persists-even-as-americans-with-lower-incomes-make-gains-in-tech-adoption/

Vyas, Lina (2022). "New normal" at work in a post-COVID world: Work – life balance and labor markets. *Policy and Society, 41*(1), 155–167.

World Health Organization. (2022). *WHO coronavirus (COVID-19) dashboard.* Retrieved from https://covid19.who.int/?mapFilter=deaths

Yavorsky, Jill E., Qian, Yue, & Sargent, Amanda C. (2021). The gendered pandemic: The implications of COVID-19 for work and family. *Sociology Compass 15*(6), e12881-n/a.

5 Intersectional Disparities During Crisis

Improving Social Equity Through Public and Nonprofit Management

Schnequa N. Diggs, Rosa Castillo Krewson, and Sean A. McCandless

Introduction

Public administration, as a discipline and a practice, has been slow to acknowledge the need to consider the differential impacts of policy and administration on populations; especially when such impacts are due to discriminatory administrative actions and policies toward race, gender identity, sexual orientation, and other social descriptors that diminish access to opportunities. Such understanding is critical because in many administrative contexts, specifically during crisis, not everyone is treated fairly – some identities are privileged while others are marginalized. Further, public administration is only beginning to gain awareness of the need for intersectional analysis to examine policy and administrative action. Put simply, intersectionality is the notion that multiple identities and status combine to inform social position resulting in inequitable policy treatment and outcomes.

At its core, public administration is focused on the public interest. Public sector bureaucracy is the vehicle for translating our laws and policies into action, managing implementation, and ensuring this is done in the best interests of the public and within constitutional governing principles of their respective nations. Within the United States, the execution of public administration has long been guided by three main pillars: economy, efficiency, and effectiveness. More recently, a fourth pillar has emerged as central to a values driven public sector – that of social equity (Norman-Major, 2011). This new pillar expands the focus and expectations for the public sector to include an active commitment to fairness, justice, and equality in the formulation and implementation of public policy, distribution of public services, and management of all institutions serving the public directly or by contract

DOI: 10.4324/9781003184621-5

(Johnson & Svara, 2015). In essence, social equity argues that attention to how administration and bureaucracy impacts all citizens is part of our administrative social contract (Guy & McCandless, 2020).

Crisis can be interpreted in many ways, ranging from a more traditional focus on natural disasters, the current global pandemic, or famines, to an expanding of crisis revolving around sudden transformations, such as violent government regime change, or even dramatic shifts in social issues such as the #MeToo and Black Lives Matter movements. For many (if not all) of these interpretations, the public sector, including both governmental and nonprofits, plays a unique role as the leader in instigating immediate responses to needs. Crisis situations often require broad and wide-ranging responses that usually necessitate action without an immediate concern for the financial bottom line. Responding to crisis also entails interacting with individuals and entities at their most vulnerable, thereby adding a moral and ethical component to fairness and equity in service provision.

It is imperative that administrators use an intersectional lens to better understand the unique experiences of people who identify with multiple identities, and how these identities influence their interactions with government agents and nonprofit organizations (Alexander & Stivers, 2010; Bishu, 2020; Blessett, 2020; Crenshaw, 1991; Guy & McCandless, 2020; Heckler & Starke, 2020; Diggs, 2022). Thus, intersectionality is a social equity issue that must be considered when examining public service responses to crisis. This chapter employs an intersectional lens within the context of social equity to make the link between systemic conditions driving inequitable distribution of harm – psychosocial, economic, or physical – to marginalized communities during crisis. Guy and McCandless (2020) describe one interpretation of social equity as "an activist notion that requires . . . [the public sector] be a lever for change" (p. 1). We assert intersectionality is a necessity for true social equity and urge public administrators to do the same. Failure to do so undermines the ability of the public sector to provide efficient, effective, or equitable services, most particularly in times of crisis.

This chapter frames how inequities occur in crisis management in three major ways. First, we offer a high-level view of intersectional inequity during crisis with particular focus on examining how and why such inequities occur. Second, we examine public sector organizations and frame the discussion largely through law, politics, and management. Third, we apply intersectionality during crisis in nonprofit organizations to uncover how nonprofits reinforce the status quo with a special focus on race, leadership, and nonprofit collaborative strategies. Following these analyses, we suggest promising strategies to foster equity and advance the study of intersectionality in public administration.

Intersectional Inequities During Crisis

Historically, public administration has worked to privilege particular identities – white, cis-gendered, heterosexual, and male – above all others. During crisis the potential is greater that existing structural inequities, prejudices, and discrimination can result in harm or even death for those with any one or combination of marginalized identities. Such inequities are additionally problematic in that public services (regardless of the sector the service is produced) should be efficient, effective, economical, and socially equitable (Blessett, 2015; Bonilla-Silva, 2003; Bullard & Wright, 2012; Gaynor & Wilson, 2020; Hooker, 2020; Kagan, 2020; Ronquillo, 2020; Wright & Merritt, 2020). To this point, intersectional inequities, during crisis, do not "just happen." Rather, inequities occur due to overlapping legal, political, and managerial reasons that function as multipliers of marginalization during crisis.

Literature on crisis has provided several definitions that reference triggering events of threat, urgency, and uncertainty. In general, crises are low frequency, high impact events that negatively impact the normal operations of government agencies, nonprofits, private institutions, and peoples' lives. These conditions may render temporal, spatial, and situational vulnerabilities on individuals and groups and their ability to access, or have control over, different types of resources (Kuran et al., 2020). Crisis can be categorized as human-caused, naturally-caused, or some combination of the two (Haddow, Bullock, & Coppola, 2020). Within the past several years, the United States has encountered numerous overlapping crises impacting public sector interventions and action. The most recent example is the overlapping events of COVID-19, political unrest following the 2020 elections, the public display of Black Americans killed by law enforcement, and hate crimes against Asian Americans.

One lesson of intersectionality scholarship is that crises reveal the existing social cleavages based upon privilege (Bullard & Wright, 2012; Crenshaw, 1991; Gaynor & Blessett, 2021; McCandless & Elias, 2021). These privileges are often situated within institutional racism that provides structural foundations resulting in ongoing barriers and inequities. Institutional racism means that institutions either do not actively work to dismantle existing racist systems (thereby perpetuating them) or do not work to challenge such systems, which results in a form of promotion of racism in both policy and practice. As such, Black, Indigenous, and People of Color (BIPOC) are seen and treated as less, despite laws and policies mandating otherwise. And when a system experiences a shock, such institutions respond in prejudiced and discriminatory ways. Given historic inequities – namely prejudice and discrimination against race, skin color, gender identity, sexual orientation, economic class, and much more – institutions do not serve everyone fairly. For instance, the experiences of cisgendered, heterosexual, white, *urban* males will differ from the experiences of cisgendered, heterosexual, white, *rural* males. When considering historically marginalized identities, especially when multiple subordinate identities combine, the outcomes differ even further. That is, those who tend to experience more costs versus benefits of public policies and administrative actions, especially during crisis, are those who already experience prejudice and discrimination against one or more of the historically marginalized identities they possess. The potential for inequity can be extensive given how numerous players are involved in any crisis, like levels and branches of government, nonprofits, businesses (large and small), community organizations, community members, and more (Bonilla-Silva, 2003; Bullard & Wright, 2012; Gaynor, 2018; Guy & McCandless, 2020; Starke, Heckler, & Mackey, 2018).

Managing crisis is itself an intersectoral endeavor, in that public, nonprofit, and private sectors are generally involved, either as individual entities or as partners to meet urgent needs. Policy decisions are made under conditions of scientific uncertainty, significant time pressure, minimal quality evidence, and often among disagreements in expert opinion on methods and directions for action (Berger et al., 2020). Historically marginalized populations are often insufficiently represented in decision-making, restricted from seats at the table, or have their concerns overlooked. The COVID-19 pandemic is an example of how crisis, in tandem with existing institutional inequities, results in intersectional inequities. BIPOC populations are more likely to contract COVID-19 and experience the worst health, economic, and longitudinal effects (Wright & Merritt, 2020). These inequities also affect vaccine access through which BIPOC populations remain under-vaccinated. Vaccine hesitancy is heightened for BIPOC populations, likely grounded in administrative racism such as the Tuskegee Experiments (Starke et al., 2018) – but this hesitancy only explains part of these dynamics. Vaccine access inequities – such as lack of transportation options, little or no information created for historically marginalized populations, vaccination sites being unknown and/or inaccessible to BIPOC populations, urban and rural divides, information technology divides; and more – result in outcome inequities. The most positive instances of BIPOC populations working to address equity in crisis have been in instances where governments and nonprofits work together to create policies, procedures, and programs to foster equity and trust. One example is community vaccination clinics and centers (CVCs), which are intersectoral collaborations that are set up in and run with the cooperation of trusted local community members to promote vaccine equity (Abdul-Mutakabbir et al., 2021; Centers for Disease Control and Prevention [CDC], 2021).

Therefore, an intersectional lens allows for a fuller understanding of inequities, discrimination, and prejudice during crisis. It also informs how social groups are both affected by, and have an effect on, the impact of various crises (Kuran et al., 2020). Through an intersectional lens, public service institutions are better positioned to provide public service equity for everyone.

Intersectionality & Crisis: The Public Sector

Historically, the provision of public services has mostly been associated with the public sector. Traditional understandings of public administration center legislative bodies as the creators of public policy and those in executive branches, regardless of government level, as the implementers of that policy. Such views are anachronistic – current views acknowledge that public administration as an inter-branch (i.e., legislative, executive, and judicial), inter-governmental (i.e., multiple levels of government), and inter-sectoral (i.e., public, nonprofit, and private) endeavor (Miller, Barnes, & Katzmann, 2004; Rosenbloom, Kravchuk, & Clerkin, 2008), especially during crisis (Haddow et al., 2020).

Intersectional governance is a term used to broadly describe the management of partnerships and cooperation between organizations in different sectors of society – nonprofits, local government, and business (Klein & McGahan, 2021; Leach & Crichlow, 2020). This is an increasingly common strategy in the public sector, but becomes of extreme importance during crisis. In these situations, the scope and scale of government may be advantageous in terms of the financial, structural, and human capital capacity. On the other hand, government action is often accompanied by the stereotypical challenges associated with bureaucracy and red tape. Nonprofit organizations, which by their very nature are not government, are often more prepared to adapt to rapid change caused by crisis or in responding to crisis. While government entities are legally required to address the needs of all, nonprofits are able to focus on more narrowly defined missions and/or populations. Financial considerations are a key difference between government and nonprofit capabilities. Nonprofits are often forced to deal with the twin challenges of increased demand for services at the same time they may have decreased resources, thus impacting their ability to adapt or rapidly respond to crisis. Arik, Clark, and Raffo (2016) asserted that during economic downturn, nonprofit organizations feel the impact more acutely compared to public and private sectors for this very reason. Since nonprofits operate within open systems, they match internal structures to prevailing environmental demands (Horvath, Brandtner, & Powell, 2018).

Legal Dimensions of Intersectionality

When examining the role of the public sector regarding intersectional inequities during crisis, it is essential to examine legal foundations. This section examines the roles of public sector (government and nonprofit) institutions in fostering and addressing legal and structural developments impacting intersectional inequities.

In the United States, government has a particularly critical role because it constitutionally and legally has numerous monopolies, such as being representative of the will of "the people" and that the US Constitution is the supreme law of the land, as per the Supremacy Clause of Article VI. In this way, constitutional and legal dimensions form baselines for understanding what governments are legally obligated to do and to protect (Miller et al., 2004; Rosenbloom et al., 2008).

From an intersectional perspective, the US Constitution originally privileged solely white, male property owners. Successive amendments, laws, and court rulings have given greater *de jure* liberties (see Table 5.1). State constitutions and laws have seen similar developments, although legal regimes across the states can and do differ in terms of who is protected, for what, and how, and issues like voter suppression prevent the full realization of equity in enfranchisement (McCandless, 2021). Constitutional amendments on the federal level have led to many statutory and case law revisions through the years, perhaps most notably demonstrated by the Civil Rights Act of 1964 which outlawed discrimination based upon race, color, religion, sex, and national origin. Recent decades have seen expansive changes and legal/legislative battlegrounds in regards to LGBTQ+, sexual orientation,

Table 5.1 Evolving Statutory and Case Law Changes

Year	Legal Action	Mandate	Demographic Focus
1865	13th Amendment	Forbade slavery	Race
1868	14th Amendment	Apply Bill of Rights to states, due process/equal protection	All "persons"
1870	15th Amendment	Enfranchisement (voting)	Gender (ALL men)
1920	19th Amendment	Enfranchisement (voting)	Gender (women)
1964	24th Amendment	Abolish poll taxes	Race
1964	Civil Rights Act	Outlaw discrimination	Race, color, religion, sex, & national origin
1971	26th Amendment	Enfranchisement (voting)	Age (for those 18+)
2019	Bostock v Clayton County	Expand Civil Rights Act protections	Sexual orientation & gender identity

and gender identity (McCandless & Elias, 2021). Legislative changes in these areas are constantly ebbing and flowing as the political scene changes, but are currently an area of significant legal shifts revolving around SCOTUS rulings in 2022.

In this way, US governments have been increasingly mandated to promote fairness for all. Still, inequities persist, and empirically documented inequities are evident across a host of political and administrative domains. Such inequities are too numerous to discuss here, but, in essence, extensive inequities remain despite enormous constitutional and legal advancements (Gooden, 2014, 2015).

Representative Dimensions of Intersectionality

From a public administration perspective, it is within public sector institutions and the management of these institutions that the realities of how and why intersectional inequities occur (Bullard & Wright, 2012; Kettl, 2020). The political dimensions of government decision-making continue to marginalize groups. It takes consensus and power to pass any law. In the policy process, laws explicitly centered on protecting the lives of historically marginalized populations can be difficult to pass. During crises, legislatures can act quickly to appropriate resources, pass new laws, and help mobilize others. However, what legislatures ultimately pass reflect decision-makers' values and beliefs. If decision-makers are unrepresentative of a population and/or think that a problem is defined a particular way, and/or believe that a population is deviant, they are unlikely to pass policies in favor of assigning benefits to marginalized groups or sufficiently factor in their needs. Further, decision-making bodies can experience deadlock when numerous interpretations of a problem are evident. The result is often little or no action, and if there is action, it is often symbolic. Widespread legal and political change to promote equity is rare, including in response to crisis (Gaynor, 2018; McCandless & Blessett, 2022; Stone, 2011).

During crisis, public agencies must determine how to respond, especially through identifying where to act, how to allocate resources, who to engage (e.g., other agencies, community groups, elected leaders), and more. Administrators' decisions, especially during crisis, have often resulted in inequities. When public systems do not prioritize the experiences and identities of historically marginalized populations, existing cleavages and inequities are exacerbated. Meaning that those at the intersections of marginalized identities are more likely to experience the most negative outcomes, whether significant harm to life, limb, property, and death (Berry-James et al., 2021; Bullard & Wright, 2012; Lewis-Ragland, 2021).

The causes of such inequities *are* understood. The problem is not with understanding the causes of inequities but in public sector agencies and agents admitting their culpability (Alkadry & Blessett, 2010; Gooden, 2014, 2015). The social construction framework helps parse these dimensions. In short, public-sector agencies are societal microcosms, and when particular groups are socially constructed negatively and have little political power, policies will assign these groups more costs than benefits (Schneider & Ingram, 1993). In public sector responses to crisis, the needs of those with the most privilege are often prioritized first and the most likely to be meaningfully addressed.

The reasons why inequities persist and are exacerbated during crisis are becoming better understood. Bolman and Deal's (2017) four-part frame of organizations helps parse the various ways in which inequitable crisis management manifests – structure, human resources, politics, and symbolism. Using this framework, public sector organizations' structures exacerbate intersectional inequities during crisis. A central reason is that organizations' work depends upon information. Information during crisis must flow upward, downward, horizontally, and in increasingly networked ways. On the whole, information regarding the effects of crisis on historically marginalized populations frequently does not get noticed by decision-making authorities. Sometimes the information is not transferred correctly, and communication with privileged actors becomes prioritized (Gaynor & Wilson, 2020; Headley, 2020; McCandless, 2018). Nonprofits serve a crucial role in this regard through their outsider role: they bring new avenues of communication outside of traditional channels, they provide outlets for marginalized voices, and often highlight innovative, dynamic, or even contradictory viewpoints (Wright & Merritt, 2020).

Within the human resources frame, representative bureaucracy theory argues that public sector organizations are better able to serve historically marginalized groups when agencies are representative of the populations they serve (Elias, 2013). Even when bureaucrats are not members of historically marginalized populations, they can still advocate for equity. Still, many agencies tend to be unrepresentative. Despite improvements, BIPOC populations and women are underrepresented in government, particularly in top-level positions (Borry, Getha-Taylor, & Holmes, 2021). Women have made greater strides in breaking through the glass ceiling for senior positions in the nonprofit sector, but these inroads are mainly limited to white women, and are more evident in smaller nonprofits (Evans & Knepper, 2022). Thus, government often continues to be overwhelmingly led by those people from groups with the most privileged identities, often resulting in crisis management insufficiently addressing all groups' needs (Bishu, 2020; Hooker, 2020; Riccucci, 2015).

Politically, workforces that reflect the population they serve may help mitigate situations that can produce inequities, such as the rich and powerful having special access leading to disproportionate attention and benefits at the expense of those who may be the most in need of assistance. Historically, governments varied in terms of community outreach. Only recently have governments begun promoting equity through adopting policies and procedures centering the experiences, voices, and decision-making of historically marginalized populations. Additionally, organizational cleavages can result in battles between different groups in that groups within organizations can and do differ in terms of what is and what is not a problem. Power within different agency groups privileges *who* defines what a problem is, which then sets the stage for *what* a problem is, how viable solutions are determined, and what is ultimately enacted (Gooden, 2014; McCandless, 2018; Norman-Major & Wooldridge, 2015).

The power of symbolism often manifests in the myth of bureaucratic neutrality. Public institutions assert they serve everyone equally. The problem is that equal treatment (i.e., everyone gets the same thing) is not fair treatment because equality, ironically, often translates to historically marginalized populations experiencing harm. A related dynamic is the symbolism of agencies "not seeing race" or "not seeing gender" but that typically means in practice that inequities are often not admitted (Gooden, 2014; Guy & McCandless, 2020; Heckler, 2017; Portillo, Bearfield, & Humphrey, 2019).

Thus, agencies exacerbate intersectional inequities. In brief, they adopt strategies maintaining the status quo (whether through ignoring or insufficiently admitting a problem), fail to define issues affecting historically marginalized populations as problems, do little to help marginalized populations address problems, or even tell historically marginalized groups that they are wrong about the existence of or need to address an inequity (McCandless & Blessett, 2022).

Intersectionality and Crisis: The Nonprofit Sector

Crisis presents a forced, but unique, opportunity for nonprofits to shape and rethink how they go about their missions, how they operate in constrained funding periods, who they engage with in the community, and how they engage, all of which impact their decision-making process. Nonprofit board members and executives need to reflect on and challenge dominant power dynamics influenced by preconceived notions of leadership and intersecting social inequities in order to build innovative, creative organizations that can adapt to changing environments and climates. Applying an intersectional equity lens can empower nonprofits to alter how they respond to crisis in practical ways. To this end, change in the nonprofit sector is both change in the wider institutional environment in which nonprofits operate and within the organizations themselves (Horvath et al., 2018).

Much like the public sector, nonprofit organizations are not immune to the oppressive forces that shape institutional structures, decision-making, and organizational culture (Nickels & Leach, 2021). Many local nonprofits work to serve the most vulnerable and marginalized groups within the population. Nonprofit organizations hold a special place in society as they were often created to fill gaps in services provided by the government and the private sector. Yet, these same organizations are neither representative of, nor have the contextual knowledge needed to understand the social experiences of the clients they serve (Nickels & Leach, 2021). This is also apparent when the mission of the organization has a social justice or social equity focus (Heckler, 2019; Kunreuther & Thomas-Breitfeld, 2020). Homogenized organizations and organizational practices fundamentally lack consideration of intersectionality and the nuanced perspectives lend to the understanding of vulnerable and historically marginalized groups. Without regard, nonprofits preserve pre-crisis social, economic, and cultural factors that inform inequality, exclusion, and access to viable resources, which becomes especially apparent in crisis (Kuran et al., 2020).

Intersectionality of race and leadership in nonprofits are rarely discussed in the literature, especially when considering the effects of crisis. Studies on race and nonprofit leadership have shown that very few people of color are able to move into positions of leadership (Fredette & Bernstein, 2019; Griffin, 2021; Heckler, 2019). Disparate patterns within the nonprofit leadership mirror racialized and gendered spaces (Nickels & Leach, 2021). The overrepresentation of White males in leadership, privileges the voices of the dominant group in decision making while excluding the voices of those directly affected by the issues. This example of paternalism grants service delivery and program decisions to outsiders who make decisions on behalf of the communities and people in need, commonly referred to as White-savior syndrome (Nickels & Leach, 2021), which essentially ignores the knowledge of community members.

From an intersectional perspective, Anderson (2015) depicts nonprofits as White spaces where "Whiteness" is privileged and maintained through norms, values, and performance that reinforce the status quo. For Heckler (2017, 2019), Whiteness is a realized public value embedded in nonprofit organizations through informal and formal rules, norms, and culture. Both authors point to the issue of "Whiteness" functioning as the standard in which all other categories are implicitly compared (Emirbayer & Desmond, 2012). This realization asserts that privilege is assigned to Whiteness or White racial identity and used to devise social hierarchies, societal dynamics (Diggs, 2021), racial power dynamics (Leach & Crichlow, 2020), and drive performance and funding outcomes (Nickel & Leach, 2021) for nonprofits, thereby undermining an equitable intersectional approach.

During crisis, nonprofits often adopt practices encouraged by funders, governing boards, and government (whose power is derived from maintaining the status quo) in responding to urgent financial or service demands. The power these entities have on agenda setting, organizational strategy, and policy implementation is a testament to the privileged dominant groups who hold these positions. These individuals [White males] are best positioned to inform fiduciary needs by shaping the problem and solutions from an advantaged point. As such, racial disparities in nonprofit leadership also frame the differential impacts of power relations within intersectional governance (Leach & Crichlow, 2020), thus impacting their ability to respond equitably in crisis situations.

Underlying racial power dynamics also takes shape when determining which nonprofit organizations are likely to receive competitive financial support. Thompson (2012) argues that the disparities in funding directed toward minority-run and minority-serving nonprofit organizations stems from historical discrimination and can be traced back to the lack of relationships with primarily White foundation decision-makers. This is particularly alarming for prospective minority organizational leaders who encounter challenges establishing relationships with potential funders. If race and gender are continuously assigned to executive leadership and fiduciary responsibilities, nonprofit organizations will continue to be reluctant to advance individuals who identify with intersectional identities (i.e. women of color) into leadership which perpetuates the status quo.

Public Sector Management Strategies for Equity

Recognizing and addressing intersectional identities and their impacts is crucial to fulfilling the values inherent in social equity within the government and nonprofit sectors. This is exponentially more important to address when dealing with crisis situations that compound the inequities for intersectional and marginalized populations. Public sector organizations can undertake several strategies to better address intersectional inequities during crisis in their management practices, thus improving public service provision in the core pillars of economy, efficiency, and effectiveness, as well as the more recent social equity pillar. These strategies will help ensure social equity accountability and the development and implementation of policies that are fair for all. Perhaps most imperatively, strategies need to be implemented before crises, not just during or after. Having leaders who take the time to recognize, understand, engage, prioritize, and evaluate is a necessary foundation for organizations that wish to move beyond mere symbolic efforts and achieve substantive change. Organizations, and their leaders, need to expand outreach and collaborations – internally with employees, with their clients and stakeholders, with other organizations, and inter-sectorally.

Spotlight Box: Changing Dynamics in Public Sector Organizations

Federal Emergency Management Agency [FEMA] – coordinates crisis and disaster responses in the US, including distributing emergency funding to states. In recent years, FEMA (2021) has worked to foster awareness and education of equitable practices and recognize equity and inclusion as a continuous process. They have worked to partner with local community-based organizations, thereby expanding the range of voices and experiences in the decision-making process. FEMA has worked to expand their understanding of historical and cultural foundations that have so often led to "underinvestment, disinvestment, and destructive policies" that so often have resulted in policies favoring affluent, white communities at the expense of historically marginalized communities (p. 10).

The *Georgetown Climate Center* (GCC, 2021) focuses on three overarching goals for intersectional equity, namely involving community members (especially "frontline" community members) in decision-making about developing, implementing, and evaluating disaster and crisis preparedness strategies. The importance is to make such strategies align with communities' needs and values. Other strategies include minimizing consequences of crisis for low-income communities by ensuring equitable access to resources, locating crisis assistance programs directly in frontline communities, working to prevent communities from being uprooted due to crisis, and collaborating with the affected community members to develop solutions.

Collaboration opens the door and brings new voices, experiences, and ideas to the table. But, collaboration requires an organizational structure and culture that are open to change. Organizational cultures are driven by the values, beliefs, and norms within the respective organization, and often serve as an indoctrination mechanism. Cultures can perpetuate existing ways of thinking and practice by assimilating new individuals into existing patterns. However, organizational cultures that value the intersectional dynamics of their workforce can be a valuable tool for change by "valuing creativity and tolerance of creative people, believing that innovating and acting boldly to seize opportunities are appropriate behaviors to deal with survival and environmental uncertainty" (McGuire, 2003, p. 6).

Public and nonprofit organizations can better position themselves to deal with future crisis situations by creating organizational structures and policies that provide room for adaptation and flexibility. This must be paired with the recruitment of leaders that have management styles capable of adjusting to rapidly changing dynamics and situations and that work toward fostering organizational cultures that value creativity, innovation, and outside the box thinking. This will allow organizations to move from what Miles and Snow (2003) call a "reactor" environment into a "prospector" mentality that embraces new technologies, innovation, and willingness to take risks in pursuit of long-term success. Similarly, Miles and Snow (2003) use the term "analyzer" to classify organizations open to change but hesitant for this large of a step, instead taking more cautious steps and making incremental changes in technology and programs after observing successes or failures by their prospector counterparts. In terms of crisis preparation, what is essential is to avoid being a "defender" organization that continues with the status quo, refusing to deviate from their core mission, and continually focused on efficiency in current practices and programs and reluctant to change or innovate, resulting in the perpetuation of status quo inequities.

Much of the business management and public administration literature supports the idea that organizations can enhance their performance when strategy and structure are in alignment (Miles & Snow, 2003; Dusya & Crossan, 2004). However, when organizational culture and strategy are misaligned, the organization will not operate as efficiently, and a specific type of leader will be needed to realign the organization. This is a daunting challenge because, although important, organizational culture is very difficult to change. One method of changing directions is reworking the recruitment and retention process, thus providing opportunities for outreach beyond the traditional pools of candidates into new, intersectional demographics, new ways of thinking, and new insights into how missions and programs will impact communities. But these changes will not happen on their own, they require intentional efforts and support from all levels of organizations (workers, leaders, and board). Without these efforts, public sector organizations will continue on the path of hegemony of Whiteness and masculinity in executive leadership and reinforcing the status quo.

Organizational shifts in personnel must be matched with shifts in the organizational culture to ensure a welcoming and inclusive environment, including changes in underlying assumptions about individuals or groups that may provide unspoken barriers for advancement. For instance, Kunreuther and Thomas-Breitfield (2020) assert people of color have been perceived by some in the status quo as "troublemakers" rather than as innovators seeking to create bold changes in a way an organization carries out its mission. These types of misperceptions undermine the ability of organizations to adapt, innovate, or prepare for either crisis or simply day-to-day survival in constantly changing environments.

Studies have demonstrated that people of color in organizations are just as qualified as their White peers who advance to leadership positions, but this has not been matched in demographic statistics for senior executive or board positions in the public sector (Boyarski, 2018; Kunreuther & Thomas-Breitfeld, 2020). Kunreuther and Thomas-Beitfield's 2016 *Race to Lead* report suggests that ongoing racialized barriers and oppressive organizational cultures often hinder people of color's advancement into leadership. To counter the oppressive voice within dominant narratives, organizations can employ counter-narratives as a method of resistance, which are designed to shift organizational culture. This requires an organizational openness, both structurally and as part of leadership efforts, to intentionally incorporate a broader range of narratives that include BIPOC and intersectional narratives and life experiences (Solorzano & Yosso, 2001, p. 3). This approach counters the reproduction of existing hegemony of executive leadership by casting doubt and prompts critique of the views held by the White male public sector leaders (Delgado & Stefanic, 2017).

Blessett, Gaynor, Witt, and Alkadry (2016) suggest that counter-narratives can be used to challenge "the status quo with respect to thinking about, understanding, and developing solutions to address social ills" (p. 270) in nonprofit spaces, and opening the door for innovative change and outside the box thinking. Taken together, "drawing upon the epistemic advantage of marginalized or muted voices, begins the process of dismantling the inviolability of White masculine [public sector] spaces" (Nickels & Leach, 2021 p. 524).

These ideas aren't just extensions of "woke" efforts to increase diversity, equity, or inclusion (DEI). They are, at their core, good management practices. Similar to representative bureaucracy theory for government personnel, research has shown that diversity in nonprofit leadership, particularly when that diversity is representative of the clients served, increases responsiveness to or convergence with clients' needs and fulfillment of mission focus as well as improving performance expectations by community stakeholders (LeRoux, 2009; Fredette & Bernstein, 2019). In other words, leveraging intersectionality as a strategy to foster equity in public sector management will lead to more inclusive and just workplaces and service provision, specifically during times of crisis.

Conclusion

Improving public sector practice and fulfilling the values inherent in social equity begins with admitting issues and understanding how and why intersectional inequities occur, especially through admitting institutional culpability. Relatedly, agencies must understand, center, and act upon the experiences of historically marginalized groups, especially through fostering meaningful seats at the table. Public sector organizations must also diversely, inclusively, equitably, and democratically determine what fairness means, how to achieve it, as well as how to measure success (Alkadry & Blessett, 2010; Blessett, 2020; Johnson & Svara, 2015).

Throughout, public sector agencies must acknowledge the multidimensionality of identity and status. Policies and administrative practices have often treated identity as static or as single categories. It is difficult but necessary to acknowledge that statuses and experiences combine as well as differ. Whatever public sector organizations do, they need to consider how a social equity focus results in better practice and that equity is only equitable if it is intersectional. In many ways, the lack of considering intersectionality within the context of social equity is a form of crisis within itself. Any administrative or policy action will differentially affect groups based upon prejudice and discrimination (or lack thereof) directed at any one or combination of identities. This is why public sector government policies and procedures require constant revision and tweaking and learning. As a baseline, social equity must become part of the repertoire in public sector management (Gaynor, 2018; Gaynor & Blessett, 2021; Headley, 2020; Heckler & Starke, 2020; Larson, 2020).

Public administration has a long way to go to better understand, incorporate, and equitably act upon knowledge of intersectionality, especially during crisis. As shown in the discussion above, an intersectional lens is essential to understand differential impacts of crisis on historically marginalized populations, especially concerning the equity of public services, such as in access, processes, quality, and outcomes. Despite increasing emphasis on social equity in the public sector and growing protections implicating fairness, governance policies and practices remain prejudicial and discriminatory, and during crises, existing inequities are exacerbated while new ones are created. In the public sector, the causes of intersectional inequities are extensive and occur especially in the management of such institutions. In terms of nonprofits, executive leadership continues to lack in diversity and is matched by limited research on intersectionality or models for leading successful organizational change grounded in social equity.

However, promising strategies are evident. These include agencies admitting challenges, engaging in extensive outreach with historically marginalized populations, centering and valuing the lives and experiences of marginalized populations, and adopting specific strategies to promote accountability for social equity. With these dimensions better understood and acted upon, both the public and nonprofit sectors will be better placed to ameliorate inequities *before* crisis so that the intersectional inequities that can and do occur *during* crisis are equitably and fairly addressed so that all populations get the resources they need to resiliently rebuild.

References

Abdul-Mutakabbir, Jacinda C., Casey, Samuel, Jews, Veatrice, King, Andrea, Simmons, Kelvin, Hogue, Michael D., . . . Veltman, Jennifer (2021). A three-tiered approach to address barriers to COVID-19 vaccine delivery in the Black community. *The Lancet, 9*(6), e749–e750.

Alexander, Jennifer, & Stivers, Camilla (2010). An ethic of race for public administration. *Administrative Theory & Praxis, 32*(4), 578–597.

Alkadry, Mohamad G. & Blessett, Brandi (2010). Aloofness or dirty hands? Administrative culpability in the making of the second ghetto. *Administrative Theory and Praxis, 32*(4), 532–556.

Anderson, Elijah (2015). The white space. *Sociology of Race and Ethnicity, 1*(1), 10–21.

Arik, Murat, Clark, Leigh A., and Raffo, Deana M. (2016). Strategic responses on non-profit organizations to the economic crisis: Examining through the lenses of resource dependency and resourced-based view theories. *Academy of Strategic Management Journal, 15*(1), 48–70.

Berger, Loïc, Berger, Nicolas, Bosetti, Valentina, Gilboa, Itzhak, Hansen, Lars P., Jarvis, Christopher, Marinacci, Massimo, & Smith, Richard D. (2020). Uncertainty and decision-making during a crisis: How to make policy decisions in the COVID-19 context? University of Chicago, Becker Friedman Institute for Economics Working Paper, (2020–95).

Berry-James, RaJade M., Blessett, Brandi, Emas, Rachel, McCandless, Sean, Nickels, Ashley E., Norman-Major, Kristen, & Vinzant, Parisa (2021). Stepping up to the plate: Making social equity a priority in public administration's troubled times. *Journal of Public Affairs Education, 27*(1), 5–15.

Bishu, Sebawit G. (2020). Gender equity in the workplace. In M. E. Guy & S. A. McCandless (Eds.), *Achieving social equity: From problems to solutions* (pp. 15–27). Irvine, CA: Melvin & Leigh.

Blessett, Brandi (2015). Disenfranchisement: Historical underpinnings and contemporary manifestations. *Public Administration Quarterly, 39*(1), 3–50.

Blessett, Brandi (2020). Rethinking the administrative state through an intersectional framework. *Administrative Theory & Praxis, 42*(1), 1–5.

Blessett, Brandi, Gaynor, Tia S., Witt, Matthew, & Alkadry, Mohamad G. (2016). Counter-narratives as critical perspectives in public administration curricula. *Administrative Theory & Praxis, 38*(4), 267–284.

Bolman, Lee G., & Deal, Terrence E. (2017). *Reframing organizations: Artistry, choice, and leadership* (6th ed). New York: John Wiley & Sons.

Bonilla-Silva, Eduardo (2003). *Racism without racists: Color-blind racism and the persistence of racial inequality in the United States.* Lanham, MD: Roman & Littlefield Publishers.

Borry, Erin L., Getha-Taylor, Heather, & Holmes, Maja H. (2021). Promoting diversity and inclusion in the federal workforce: Executive Order 13583 and demographic trends. *Public Administration Quarterly, 45*(4), 392–417.

Boyarski, Luisa (2018). Advancing racial equity within nonprofits: 2018 research results. In *Center for public and nonprofit leadership.* Washington, DC: Georgetown University.

Bullard, Robert D., & Wright, Beverly (2012). *The wrong complexion for protection: How the government response to disaster endangers African American Communities.* New York: NYU Press.

Centers for Disease Control and Prevention. (2021). *A guide for community partners: Increasing COVID-19 vaccine uptake among members of racial and ethnic minority communities.* Retrieved from www.cdc.gov/vaccines/covid-19/downloads/guide-community-partners.pdf

Crenshaw, Kimberlé (1991). Mapping the margins: Intersectionality, identity politics, and violence against women of color. *Stanford Law Review, 43*(6), 1241–1299.

Delgado, Richard, & Stefancic, Jean (2017). *Critical race theory: An introduction* (3rd ed.). New York: University Press.

Diggs, Schnequa N. (2021). The delusion of privilege. *Administrative Theory and Praxis, 43.*

Diggs, Schnequa N. (2022). Intersectionality of gender and race in governmental affairs. In P. Shields & N. M. Elias (Eds.), *Handbook gender in public administration* (pp. 115–132). Cheltenham, UK and Northampton, MA: Edward Elgar Publishing.

Dusya, Vera, & Crossan, Mary (2004). Strategic leadership and organizational learning. *The Academy of Management Review, 29*(2), 222–240.

Elias, Nichol M. R. (2013). Shifting diversity perspectives and new avenues for representative bureaucracy. *Public Administration Quarterly, 37*(3), 331–373.

Emirbayer, Mustafa & Desmond, Matthew (2012). Race and reflexivity. *Ethnic and Racial Studies, 35*(4), 574–599.

Evans, Michelle D., & Knepper, Hillary J. (2022). Gender and nonprofit administration: Past, present and future. In P. Shields & N. M. Elias (Eds.), *Handbook on gender and public administration* (pp. 195–211). Cheltenham, UK and Northampton, MA: Edward Elgar Publishing.

Federal Emergency Management Agency. (2021). *Building alliances for equitable resilience: Advancing equitable resilience through partnerships and diverse perspectives.* Retrieved from www.fema.gov/sites/default/files/documents/fema_rnpn_building-alliances-for-equitable-resilience.pdf

Fredette, Christopher, & Sessler Bernstein, Ruth (2019). Ethno-racial diversity on nonprofit boards: A critical mass perspective. *Nonprofit and Voluntary Sector Quarterly, 48*(5), 931–952.

Gaynor, Tia S. (2018). Social construction and the criminalization of identity: State-sanctioned oppression and an unethical administration. *Public Integrity, 20*(4), 358–369.

Gaynor, Tia S., & Blessett, Brandi (2021). Predatory policing, intersectional subjection, and the experiences of LGBTQ people of color in New Orleans. *Urban Affairs Review* [Online First].

Gaynor, Tia S., & Wilson, Meghan E. (2020). Social vulnerability and equity: The disproportionate impact of COVID-19. *Public Administration Review, 80*(5), 832–838.

Georgetown Climate Center. (2021). *Equitable disaster preparedness, response & recovery*. Retrieved from www.georgetownclimate.org/adaptation/toolkits/equitable-adaptation-toolkit/equitable-disaster-preparedness-response-recovery.html?

Gooden, Susan T. (2014). *Race and social equity: A nervous area of government*. Armonk, NY: M. E. Sharpe.

Gooden, Susan T. (2015). From equality to social equity. In M. E. Guy & M. M. Rubin (Eds.), *Public administration evolving: From foundations to the future* (pp. 209–229). New York: Routledge.

Griffin, Angela J. (2021). *A seat at the table: A phenomenological study of the gap in African American/Black women with nonprofit executive leadership roles* (Ph.D.). ProQuest Dissertations Publishing.

Guy, Mary E., & McCandless, Sean A. (2020). *Achieving social equity: From problems to solutions*. Irvine, CA: Melvin & Leigh.

Haddow, George D., Bullock, Jane A., & Coppola, Damon P. (2020). *Introduction to emergency management* (7th ed.). Oxford: Butterworth-Heinemann.

Headley, Andrea M. (2020). Race, ethnicity, and social equity in policing. In M. E. Guy & S. A. McCandless (Eds.), *Achieving social equity: From problems to solutions* (pp. 82–97). Irvine, CA: Melvin and Leigh.

Heckler, Nuri (2017). Publicly desired color-blindness: Whiteness as a realized public value. *Administrative Theory & Praxis, 39*(3), 175–192.

Heckler, Nuri (2019). Whiteness and masculinity in nonprofit organizations: Law, money, and institutional race and gender. *Administrative Theory & Praxis, 41*(3), 266–285.

Heckler, Nuri, & Starke, Anthony M. (2020). At the intersection of identities. In M. E. Guy & S. A. McCandless (Eds.), *Achieving social equity: From problems to solutions* (pp. 53–64). Irvine, CA: Melvin and Leigh.

Hooker, Jennifer (2020). LGBTQ persons, allies, and the pursuit of social equity. In M. E. Guy & S. A. McCandless (Eds.), *Achieving social equity: From problems to solutions* (pp. 28–40). Irvine, CA: Melvin and Leigh.

Horvath, Aaron, Bradtner, Christoff, & Powell, Walter W. (2018). Serve or conserve: Mission, strategy, and multi-level nonprofit change during the great recession. *Voluntas, 29*(5), 976–993.

Johnson, Norman J., & Svara, James H. (2015). Toward a more perfect union: Moving forward with social equity. In N. J. Johnson & J. H. Svara (Eds.), *Justice for all: Promoting social equity in public administration* (pp. 265–290). New York: Routledge.

Kagan, Jennifer A. (2020). Social equity and environmental justice. In M. E. Guy & S. A. McCandless (Eds.), *Achieving social equity: From problems to solutions* (pp. 142–157). Irvine, CA: Melvin and Leigh.

Kettl, Donald F. (2020). States divided: The implications of American federalism for COVID-19. *Public Administration Review, 80*(4), 595–602.

Klein, Peter G., & McGahan, Anita M. (2021). Why intersectional governance matters. In D. P. Gitterman & N. Britto (Eds.), *The intersector: How the public, nonprofit, and private sectors can address America's challenges* (pp. 21–31). Brookings Institution Press. www.brookings.edu/wp-content/uploads/2020/08/9780815739029_ch1.pdf

Kunreuther, Frances. and Thomas-Breitfield, Sean (2020). *Race to lead revisited: Obstacles and opportunities in addressing the nonprofit racial leadership gap.* New York: Building Movement Project. Retrieved from: https://buildingmovement.org/reports/race-to-lead-revisited-national-report/

Kuran, Christian H. A., Morsut, Claudia, Kruke, Bjørn I., Krüger, Marco, Segnestam, Lisa, Orru, Kati, . . . Torpan, Sten (2020). Vulnerability and vulnerable groups from an intersectionality perspective. *International Journal of Disaster Risk Reduction, 50.*

Larson, Samantha J. (2020). How transit matters for social equity. In M. E. Guy & S. A. McCandless (Eds.), *Achieving social equity: From problems to solutions* (pp. 98–111). Irvine, CA: Melvin and Leigh.

Leach, Kirk A., & Crichlow, Wesley (2020). CRT intersectionality and non-profit collaboration: A critical reflection. *Community Development Journal, 55*(1), 121–138.

LeRoux, Kelly (2009). The effects of descriptive representation on nonprofits' civic intermediary roles: A test of the "racial mismatch" hypothesis in the social services sector. *Nonprofit and Voluntary Sector Quarterly, 38*(5), 741–760.

Lewis-Ragland, Yolanda (2021). *Navigating a triple pandemic: Healthcare workers of color confront racism in America, health disparities in medicine & the trauma of COVID-19* (Vol. 1). Waterbury, CT: Joan Tomlinson Publishing.

McCandless, Sean A. (2018). Improving community relations: How police strategies to improve accountability for social equity affect citizen perceptions. *Public Integrity, 20*(4), 370–385.

McCandless, Sean A. (2021). The rule of law. *Public Integrity, 23*(1), 107–109.

McCandless, Sean A. & Blessett, Brandi (2022). Dismantling racism and white supremacy in public service organizations and society: Contextualizing the discussion and introducing the symposium. *Administrative Theory & Praxis, 44*(2), 91–104.

McCandless, Sean A., & Elias, Nicole M. (2021). Taking stock of Bostock: Implications for theory and praxis. *Administrative Theory & Praxis, 43*(1), 1–15.

McGuire, Stephen J. J. (2003). *Entrepreneurial organizational culture: Construct definition and instrument development and validation* (Ph.D.). ProQuest Dissertations Publishing.

Miles, Raymond, & Snow, Charles (2003). *Organizational strategy, structure, and process.* Stanford: Stanford University Press.

Miller, Mark C., Barnes, Jeb, & Katzmann, Robert A. (2004). *Making policy, making law: An interbranch perspective.* Georgetown: Georgetown University Press.

Nickels, Ashley E., & Leach, Kirk A. (2021). Toward a more just nonprofit sector: Leveraging a critical approach to disrupt and dismantle white masculine space. *Public Integrity, 23*(5), 515–530.

Norman-Major, Kristen (2011). Balancing the four Es; Or can we achieve equity for social equity in public administration? *Journal of Public Affairs Education, 17*(2), 233–252.

Norman-Major, Kristen, & Wooldridge, Blue (2015). Using framing theory to make the economic care for social equity: The role of policy entrepreneurs in reframing the debate. In N. J. Johnson & J. H. Svara (Eds.), *Justice for all: Promoting social equity in public administration* (pp. 209–227). New York: Routledge.

Portillo, Shannon, Bearfield, Domonic, & Humphrey, Nicole (2019). The myth of bureaucratic neutrality: Institutionalized inequity in local government hiring. *Review of Public Personnel Administration, 40*(3), 516–531.

Riccucci, Norma (2015). From sameness to differentness. In M. E. Guy & M. M. Rubin (Eds.), *Public administration evolving: From foundations to the future* (pp. 192–209). New York: Routledge.

Ronquillo, John C. (2020). Bringing first nations into the fray: Indigenous Americans and social equity. In M. E. Guy & S. A. McCandless (Eds.), *Achieving social equity: From problems to solutions* (pp. 142–157). Irvine, CA: Melvin and Leigh.

Rosenbloom, David H., Kravchuk, Robert, & Clerkin, Richard M. (2008). *Public administration: Understanding management, politics, and law in the public sector.* New York, NY: McGraw-Hill.

Schneider, Anne, & Ingram, Helen (1993). Social construction of target populations: Implications for politics and policy. *American Political Science Review, 87*(2), 334–347.

Solorzano, Daniel, & Yosso, Tara J. (2001). Critical race and LatCrit theory and method: Counter-storytelling. *International Journal of Qualitative Studies in Education, 14*(4), 471–495.

Starke, Anthony M., Heckler, Nuri, & Mackey, Janiece (2018). Administrative racism: Public administration education and race. *Journal of Public Affairs Education, 24*(4), 469–489.

Stone, Randall W. (2011). *Controlling institutions: International organizations and the global economy.* Cambridge, England: Cambridge University Press.

Thompson, Vanessa (2012). African American philanthropy: Community foundations' giving to minority-led nonprofit organizations. *SPNHA Review, 8*(1), 43–56.

Wright, James E, & Merritt, Cullen C. (2020). Social equity and COVID-19: The case of African Americans. *Public Administration Review, 80*(5), 820–826.

6 The Integrative Crisis Management Model

Michelle D. Evans, Tiffany J. Henley, and Hillary J. Knepper

Introduction

We can't escape the media. In our wired society we are no longer relegated to catching the news on our televisions or radios at set times during the day or evening. We carry it with us everywhere, from computers to mobile phones to watches. We believe society's pervasive exposure to media in real time, from around the world, gives us an unprecedented view into (in)equitable distribution of crisis management practices on a global scale. This view provides a unique opportunity for change.

By writing *Intersectionality and Crisis Management: A Path to Social Equity* we intentionally set about embedding the equity discourse into how we conceptualize crisis. For the first time, we're demonstrating that using an intersectional framework could advance the ideals and principles of equity and transform how we serve people before, during, and after crisis. This drives our premise that practitioners and scholars need new strategies to manage (and study) organizational processes, employees, and services. Our assertion is that by joining intersectionality and crisis management, we have created a platform from which to develop these new strategies. We propose the Integrative Crisis Management Model as an alternative to traditional models. Along the way, we have provided clarity among definitions of intersectionality and crisis management, considered human resource management implications, and provided examples of applications of these concepts in practice.

In this concluding chapter, we introduce our new integrative model and its relevance for the practitioner. Ultimately, we hope that we stimulate conversations and opportunities that bridge the gap between practice and theory for more informed crisis management.

DOI: 10.4324/9781003184621-6

Transformation: Introducing the Integrative Crisis Management Model

Crisis management models generally contain some iteration of these key strategic planning elements – signaling or detection, risk identification and prevention, containment, return to normal, assessment, and redesign (Fink, 1986; Mitroff, Shrivastava, & Udwadia, 1987). Burnett (1998) offers a further breakdown of what is necessary to accurately assess crisis decisions: threat level, time constraints, key decision makers, available information, and implications for actions taken. Yet, missing from each of these models is the intersectional context for analysis. Therefore, all crisis management is limited – unable to fully account for the disparate impact crisis has on people and communities as a result of their intersectional attributes. We assert a redesign of the traditional crisis management model is long overdue.

Mitroff et al. (1987) are credited with early development of crisis management models, as shown in Figure 6.1, which is adapted from their work. This is the traditional model for crisis management. Understanding how to read the five elements in Figure 6.1 is as follows: *Signal Detection* identifies potential areas of concern and risk; *Probing & Prevention* attempts to investigate and promote risk mitigation and informs preparation; *Damage Containment* works to lessen the impact of the crisis as it is happening; *Recovery* lays out steps for rebuilding, and *Assessment and Learning* analyzes effectiveness by identifying what worked and what can be done better. As you can see from the arrows in Figure 6.1, there is opportunity for feedback across these five elements of the model. We have chosen to build upon this traditional model and its continuous feedback loop because of its clarity and universality in understanding how to effectively manage crisis.

Our proposed Integrative Crisis Management Model (ICCM), depicted in Figure 6.2, offers a transformative adaptation that we believe will lead to more equitable practices. By pausing to engage in more intentional intersectional analysis, we believe planners will be able to more holistically serve their communities. The adaptation presented in Figure 6.2 activates a new framework of four constructs that can be used for improving intersectional context. This framework can lead to more integrative and comprehensive analysis, planning, and practice at key stages of crisis management.

Using Mitroff's five foundational stages of crisis management (presented in gray in Figure 6.1) – Signal Detection, Probing and Prevention, Damage Containment, Recovery, and Assessment and Learning, we overlay our intersectional framework (presented in black in Figure 6.2) to identify key stages at which we can integrate myriad community attributes and identities to guide deeper understanding of people and their communities. In turn, this could strengthen resiliency behaviors and activities. Our four essential elements of integrative activation that comprise the intersectional framework

Figure 6.1 Crisis Management Model
Source: Adapted Mitroff et al. (1987)

are: *Understanding Intersectional Constructs, Identifying Intersectional Practices, Implementing Intersectional Practices, and Reviewing Intersectional Outcomes.*

The power of this Integrative Crisis Management Model lies in its opportunity for more transparent and open discourse and acknowledgement of planning and implementation decisions and actions that fully serve, or not, the needs of communities. Through this new discourse, we can attempt to redress disparities in public service provisions. We use examples from the COVID-19 global pandemic to guide understanding of how the four intersectional elements of the integrative model provide deeper consideration for practice. Conceptually, we have engaged the five stages of crisis management where it is most crucial to step back and analyze each stage

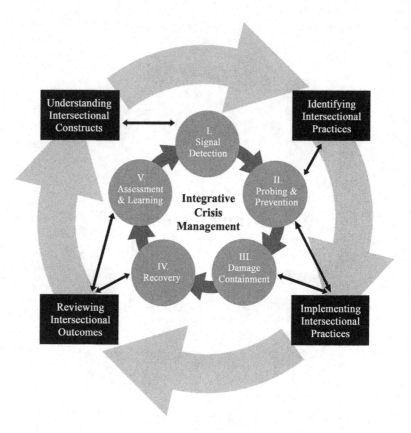

Figure 6.2 The Integrative Crisis Management Model

within the context of intersectionality. To provide further clarification, each stage is accompanied by an example to illustrate the application of the intersectional frame. It is our hope that our new integrative model, combined with the examples, will spur reflective thinking and result in more equitable practices.

Understanding Intersectional Constructs can be used at the first stage, Signal Detection, to build a more complete and equitable understanding of potential problems and risk. This is accomplished by identifying intersectional constructs that lead to problem differentiation. For example, in considering the potential challenges of a global pandemic, it was important to consider that low-income minority women work disproportionately in service jobs, placing them in riskier settings, and in turn that they would have less access to adequate personal protective equipment. *Identifying Intersectional Practices* can be applied in the second stage, Probing and Prevention. At this stage, more equitable risk mitigation and preparation practices could be identified. Examples of this could include preparing for ways to overcome a historic cultural lack of trust in healthcare providers or religious concerns with vaccination, both of which put separate communities at heightened risk. After that, *Implementing Intersectional Practices* informs Damage Containment (and provides additional feedback for Probing and Prevention). Examples here for risk mitigation include building trust between healthcare providers and individuals within targeted communities or boosting internet capacity, because education for low-income students of color was disproportionately affected during the COVID-19 pandemic (Hough, 2021). Last, Reviewing Intersectional Outcomes informs Assessment and Learning, which feeds back into improvements in managing Recovery efforts. In other words, who was most and least affected by the COVID-19 pandemic? What could have been done differently to protect neighborhoods more equitably? Did working mothers fare better in some neighborhoods and not others? Why? Assessment here can be quantitative and qualitative to dig deep into the intersectional drivers that most affected recovery efforts. The COVID-19 pandemic is a useful example of crisis to illustrate how our Integrative Crisis Management Model could yield better outcomes. This model is easily applied to other crises, such as climate change and economic recessions, and offers a disruptive perspective in crisis management. Climate change and economic recession are complex problems, and each has a long history of inequity – particularly with low income communities being less protected and at greater risk of increased adversity as a result. However, it is important to note that intersectional considerations are not limited to equity across socioeconomic differences, and in fact, the roster of intersectional attributes is dynamic. For example, the global pandemic revealed continuing inequities in other areas, including working mothers across various income levels in terms of workload, productivity, caregiving, and stress.

To illustrate the Integrative Crisis Management Model in action, we use the example of domestic violence during the COVID-19 pandemic. Domestic violence is a prime example of how the intersectional categories of difference build upon each other to compound obstacles, burdens, and outcomes. Domestic violence is generally framed as partner-on-partner violence with a gendered power dynamic with women as the victim – although this framing has evolved over time to recognize domestic violence within same-sex relationships, with male-identifying victims, and child on parent violence. The dynamics of domestic violence are strongly influenced by intersectional attributes (Understanding Intersectional Constructs), such as race, ethnicity, parental status, socioeconomic status, health/(dis)ability, among a host of others. Pandemic policies, such as stay-at-home orders, highlighted how social isolation, transportation, employment status (i.e. essential worker), whether someone had school-aged children, whether there were mental health issues, or alcoholism, or even pet ownership, were often linked to increases in domestic violence. The COVID-19 pandemic saw an increase in domestic violence statistics throughout the world (Usher, Bhullar, Durkin, Gyamfi, & Jackson, 2020), particularly in countries with strong patriarchal cultural values (Maji, Bansod, & Singh, 2022). Domestic violence is strongly linked to economic instability, child care issues, or even household chore distribution (George & Wesley, 2021). As Chapter 4 discussed, women and women of color are disproportionately represented in lower paying jobs, in limited childcare situations, and impacted by pandemic-related unemployment – with the implications of these making it more challenging to leave a domestic home situation.

Policy development and implementation (Identifying and Implementing Intersectional Practices) efforts would need to incorporate concern for issues such as overcoming vaccine hesitancy based on historical trust issues in the Black and LGBTQ+ communities, while at the same time battling long-held fears by domestic violence in attempting to reach out for help, or perhaps battling stigmas related to mental health or substance abuse issues. It is possible that men, both homosexual and heterosexual, may have worried about stigmas related to masculinity social norms, thereby reducing their willingness to seek help. Recent years have also seen calls for a shift in policies related to domestic violence shelters allowing pets, or having partnerships with animal shelters, following recognition that abusers often use violence or threats of violence against pets as control mechanisms (Newberry, 2017). George and Wesley (2021) argue for the importance of accounting for intersectional attributes, including gender, financials, health/(dis)ability, emotional/physical wellbeing, as well as cultural factors, in future domestic violence policy development. The last stage, that of Reviewing Intersectional Outcomes, would need to evaluate the role that intersectional attributes played in COVID-19 pandemic policies, such as evaluating how decisions whether to shift to remote learning, work-from-home, and social isolation in general might be linked to increases in domestic violence, especially for vulnerable populations.

We argue our innovative Integrative Crisis Management Model delivers an intersectional approach to crisis management that is essential to improve management operations and practices, especially in the era of the "*new normal.*" For example, we now see a new dependence upon remote work for some and increased worksite risk for others. We see the disparate impact of educational losses in children. And unlike generations past, we have a ubiquitous 24/7 news cycle to constantly amplify inequity amid crisis from around the globe. This affords a motivation unseen in our history as we are constantly faced with privilege and oppression and the regressive nature of disadvantage.

This new integrative management model hopes to raise awareness about these issues and provide a platform from which managers and leaders can confront these inequities. This new model combines identification and analysis of vulnerabilities and oversights, recognition of the need to analyze disparate impacts based on intersectional identities, assessments, and consideration of new approaches in policy and implementation methods moving forward, and the fortitude to move away from status quo power dynamics. For instance, post-evaluation of Hurricane Katrina and other disasters found many areas where the lack of intersectional consideration led to significant, and often deadly, impacts on physical and emotional well-being. Intersectional lessons learned included how availability of pet-friendly shelters might impact decisions to evacuate (Hunt, Bogue, & Rohrbaugh, 2012). At the same time, definitions of "family" as two parents of different genders led to same-sex families being separated during evacuations or denied housing assistance post-disaster, which were often further compounded for those dealing with HIV/AIDS, or through exclusion from faith-based services (Monroe, 2006; Stukes, 2014; see also Whetstone & Demiroz, 2023). Without discounting the magnitude of these types of negative impacts, they also have economic and efficiency impacts, much like is seen in medicine, with preventative measures and policy modifications being infinitely more beneficial than dealing with the emotional, moral, and economic after-effects.

New approaches may entail a shift away from viewing social equity efforts as a "tradeoff" to either economy or efficiency (Lebovits & Teal, 2020), and instead more as an addition or value added. Ultimately, we propose that organizations and leaders who embrace opportunities for an intersectional approach to management, particularly in times of crisis, will reap the benefits in terms of economy, efficiency, effectiveness, and most important, in terms of social equity.

The Future of Scholarship

Theoretical examination of intersectionality enhances our understanding of the world around us and facilitates our construction of knowledge (Atewologun, 2018). It is also crucial that organizations change how they conceptualize problems that affect their operations due to multiple intersecting identities and positions and reconsider how problems are addressed and solved. The chapters in this book have built upon intersectional research to provide strategies that advance equity during times of crisis.

The future of intersectionality and crisis management is very promising. Methodological approaches are capturing intersecting and overlapping social constructs through quantitative, qualitative, and mixed methods. Theobald (2017) used multi-level intersectional analysis to study direct care workers with and without migrant backgrounds and found that systemic disparities exist based on migrant status, skill, and sector. The findings also indicate that cultural differences, language barriers, prejudice, migration, and professional policies contribute to structural inequalities. Bauer and Scheim (2019) noticed that many quantitative studies on intersectionality concentrate on social inequalities across classifications of groups versus mediating factors that lead to disproportionate social outcomes. They argue that studying the effects of mediating variables such as discrimination can improve our comprehension of intersectional inequalities, determine the effect of causal processes at various intersections, and generate better hypotheses. Ding, Lu, & Riccucci (2021) examine the relationship between representative bureaucracy and organizational performance through a meta-analysis of quantitative studies. They assert that the interaction between representative bureaucracy and organizational performance leads to effectiveness and equity along with transparency and fairness. They also suggest that research on representative bureaucracy should concentrate on the intersection of multiple identities such as gender, sexual orientation, race, and ethnicity.

The Academy itself is not immune to struggles with intersectionality. How inclusive can our crisis management scholarship and practices be if we're unable to create more inclusive representativeness in the Academy? One notable illustration of this is the challenge with identifying author and scholar intersectionality. Biographical data that is publicly available generally does not clearly disclose intersectional information. For example, on a website, inclusion of a photograph may serve as a proxy for the gender with which one identifies. However, this is limited to a more binary interpretation of gender and for those who present clearly in a masculine-feminine manner. Many author and scholar attributes that would be consistent with intersectionality are not available in a searchable format. How frequently do we see a scholarly article include an author biography that notes "the author identifies as a gay white man who uses a wheelchair" or "the author identifies as a neurodiverse, able-bodied Black woman" or any other number of iterations? While these examples are purely illustrative, clearly it can be difficult to know if scholars identify as LGBTQ+, or as people with disabilities or as indigenous or several other intersectional attributes that require self-disclosure. Gender, religion, race, ethnicity, socioeconomic background, etc. are among those attributes that can be challenging to identify. Disclosure has not always been the best career move. Take for example, many early women writers who published under pen names to hide their gender (The Bronte Sisters with Charlotte as Currer, Anne as Acton, and Emily as Ellis Bell; Amantine Lucile Aurore Dupi as George Sand, Mary Ann Evans as George Eliot or Louisa May Alcott as A.M. Branard). As it turns out, those early women authors' worries remain valid today – Catherine Nichols (2015) conducted an hoc experiment where she emailed a cover letter and a few pages of her completed novel to literary agents under a man's name as well as her own and discovered that manuscripts sent under a man's name were more than eight times likelier to receive a request for the full manuscript than those sent under her own name, Catherine.

In some instances, there may be exclusion and discrimination concerns when being public and open with personal information. In other cases, the vehicle for disclosing this information is often relegated to very short biographies included in scholarly articles. Some scholars may be highly visible – using social media and websites to raise awareness and to openly share varying intersectional attributes. Others may not feel safe in their ability to disclose this information. While assumptions may be made about some of these attributes and identities, without actively and openly sharing this information, accuracy remains elusive. Another consideration may be that just because someone conducts research on indigenous cultures does not mean that person is themself indigenous. Finally, how citations are managed, both in text and in reference lists, can restrict visibility for emerging scholars, and without the use of first names, virtually no clues regarding gender identity are available. While these clues are imperfect, at least they begin to provide some enhanced visibility, particularly crucial in academic disciplines that are male dominated. The larger question remains – ensuring inclusivity across a range of intersectional attributes will better inform scholarship and practice, not only in crisis management, but in the broader academic world in general.

The Future of Practice

Managing crisis through an intersectional framework requires transformational leaders. The overlapping attributes of transformational leaders include the ability to develop a vision for the organization and to cultivate a team identity. Transformational leaders are also effective in implementing innovative initiatives, communication, delegation, and motivating employees to be agents of change (Dwiedienawati, Tjahjana, Faisal, Gandasari, & Abdinagoro, 2021). This style of leadership complements an intersectional approach to crisis management. When intersectionality is used as an analytical tool, the transition from theory to practice can be carefully designed to address social inequalities and improve business practices.

The chapters in this book provide practical strategies for practitioners, academics, and policymakers. Whetstone and Demiroz (Chapter 2) argue that leaders in disaster management need to attend to power relations during crisis and consider contextuality when creating policies and delivering services. Employers can conduct a vulnerability analysis or assessment to better understand the intersectionality of their employees, vendors, and partnerships at the organizational level and their goods, services, and target population at the service level. A vulnerability analysis will allow employers to identify opportunities to improve operational efficiencies and risks or harms that may affect employees, services, or goods. Silverio et al. (Chapter 3) propose that organizations should reframe their existing policies and embrace inclusive perspectives. They also suggest that organizations in healthcare should invest in funded research to identify underlying causes of misdiagnosis and adverse outcomes for marginalized communities. To address organizational inequities and the delivery of healthcare services, an intersectional outcome analysis can be conducted to measure the progress of the changes at the organizational and service level. Ultimately, this may result in "radically redefining" impacts that necessitate equally significant changes in management structures, styles, and applications.

Hoang et al. (Chapter 4) address intersectional human resource management (HRM) in more depth, examining and linking the macro (societal) level, meso (organizational) level, and the individual (micro) level. The authors highlight how the COVID-19 pandemic has exposed HRM policies that were outdated and out of touch when faced with an urgent crisis situation. Moving forward, organizations must embrace a reimagined approach to HRM that embraces flexibility in where we work, how we work, how we evaluate productivity, and how these elements ultimately impact advancement opportunities to ensure equity and fairness for all employees. Most importantly, HRM must embrace empathy as a core value, recognizing the disparate impacts that accompany each level of intersectional difference for employees, and creating policies and cultures that accommodate the needs of employees within their individual, intersectional needs rather than a repackaging of policies and procedures that were designed for a very different workforce and very different work environment. Utilizing an intersectional framework to assess both organizational and employee needs ensures that no one falls through the cracks. Transformational leaders are in the best position to implement these strategies in an effort to progress social equity and inclusion.

Diggs et al. (Chapter 5) suggest that organizations focus on collaborations and outreach among employees and clients to increase opportunities for expanded intersectional voices and experiences being considered, valued, and involved in the decision-making and implementation process, which ultimately will promote increased social equity and fairness in policies. They also argue that public sector organizations can enhance their performance by aligning their strategy with the organizational structure and culture and by overcoming hegemonic power dynamics and narratives that serve as barriers to a more intersectional management approach. They link their work to the evolution of laws meant to broaden fairness and equity. The realignment of organizational processes using an intersectional approach will allow organizations to analyze their policies at the meso and service level to ensure that they are neither exclusionary nor discriminatory.

Perhaps the most important contribution of this book is the development of a new crisis management model that is transformative in its integration and inclusion of varying intersectionalities. It is our hope that crisis managers will adopt this model to develop a more formalized approach to incorporating the intersectional constructs of attributes that comprise individuals and their communities. Each of the authors in this book has contributed to the relevance of these constructs in better serving society in crisis by framing key areas of opportunity to deploy intersectional analysis. The common connection that underscores each chapter is the foundational intersectional work of Crenshaw (1989, 1991, 2020) and the need to consider multiple identities and attributes as well as internal and external dynamics in society and the workplace. Ultimately, this book provides five overarching contributions to the literature and practice to help communities navigate crisis in a more equitable manner:

1. The identification of reflective discussion opportunities in this underexplored confluence of management and intersectional research and practice.
2. Recommendations for improving managers' intersectional analysis proficiency to better guide decision-making.
3. Specific recommendations for practice to help managers affect change in their organizations and communities to increase equitable practices.
4. The presentation of a new crisis management model that incorporates intersectionality with the intention of improving resilience – from planning to recovery.

Conclusion

The past 30 years have been filled with a growing understanding that intersectionality has significant implications for management. While we know a great deal about intersectionality, there is much to be done to apply it meaningfully to address social, systemic, and structural inequality. We've initiated a conversation with the Integrative Crisis Management Model in order to address inequities that are magnified during times of crisis. We recognize that socially vulnerable and marginalized populations are at risk of greater adverse outcomes during times of crisis and we offer a path toward building more equitable practices. Disease, civil unrest, urbanization, the changing nature of work, and climate change are contributing to a new normal in today's workplace. Consequently, responding to this new normal with the transformative power of an intersectional crisis management framework is necessary if we are to successfully create more inclusive and integrative policies. This idea of a *"new normal"* also needs to be focused on our educational programs, changing our approaches to pedagogy in the same ways that HR is changing their approach to telecommuting and hybrid work, to digital access, and work-life balance. Broadening our understanding of intersectionality and how it impacts performance in the classroom will help change workplace dynamics, expand networks of opportunity, and increase opportunities for collaboration and engagement, which are so often built upon foundations of trust (Henson, 2019). Ultimately, attention to these concepts can also have long-term impacts on the development and transfer of professional norms for the next generation of leaders across the practitioner and academic spectrum (Diaz-Kope, Miller-Stevens, & Henley, 2019; Elias & D'Agostino, 2019; Evans, Irizarry, & Freeman, 2022).

At the same time, we must be cautious not to equate efforts to recognize and address intersectionality within our decision-making processes as simply efforts to increase diversity and help remove obstacles for vulnerable and marginalized groups. Those efforts are absolutely laudable, but true progress will also require us to shift outdated perceptions and expectations that are so often attached to how we relate to these attributes. For instance, we have focused quite a bit on the challenges of the new normal in terms of telecommuting or hybrid work and how it impacts women disproportionately in terms of inequity in childcare and household responsibilities – regardless of income. It is equally important to recognize the deeply embedded social construction and stigmas that need to be addressed to shift these expectations – such as the sometimes unspoken judgment against, for instance, heterosexual or gay men who are actively engaged in equitable sharing of parental responsibilities, taking advantage of paternity leave, or even being involved as a troop leader for daughters involved in something like Girl Scouts. This radical redefining of how to approach crisis management will symbolically reinforce our ideals and values, help build trust within and between organizations and sectors, and facilitate interdisciplinary and intersectoral collaborations throughout civil society. In doing so we will move away from marginalization of communities, reduce the intersectional overlapping of burdens and barriers (Knepper, Sonenberg, & Levine, 2018), and establish a stronger foundation of resilience and preparedness to tackle the next crisis, be it natural disaster, global pandemic, or man-made.

Throughout this book we have discussed changing dynamics regarding the recognition of intersectionality, continually evolving definitions and expansions of cultural and social attributes, and some of the legal, social, and theoretical implications in both the academic and practitioner world. It is extremely encouraging to review the expansion of tolerance and inclusiveness and the progress that has already been made in new approaches to policy development, decision-making, and implementation, as well as the shifting narratives in social construction connected to intersectionality. At the same time, we must recognize that even the adoption of new approaches such as the Integrative Crisis Management Model does not mean it will automatically have the intended impact.

This book began by highlighting the theme that transformation can be, and is, a disruptive act – with the expected accompaniment of those who embrace change and those who are resistant. We recognize that generational shifts in social norms also play a significant role in how equity is understood and embraced as a moral obligation. To paraphrase Blessett (2020, p. 4), the integration of intersectionality in our understanding and management of crisis can be a powerful tool to "deconstruct and disarm" systemic inequalities linked to those intersectionalities. But we must also recognize that this is an ongoing process that will need to be continually addressed. We can, and should, learn from our past, develop new strategies, expand our outreach, and invite new voices into the discussions. At the same time, we must recognize that there will continue to be counter forces constantly pushing back, requiring us to continually adapt, adjust, and reimagine the possibilities – but with a vigilant eye toward building *a path to social equity*.

References

Atewologun, Doyin (2018). Intersectionality theory and practice. In *Oxford research encyclopedias, business and management*. New York: Oxford University Press.

Bauer, Greta R., & Scheim, Ayden I. (2019). Methods for analytic intercategorical intersectionality in quantitative research: Discrimination as a mediator of health inequalities. *Social Science & Medicine, 226*, 236–245.

Blessett, Brandi (2020). Rethinking the administrative state through an intersectional framework. *Administrative Theory & Praxis, 42*(1), 1–5.

Burnett, John J. (1998). A strategic approach to managing crises. *Public Relations Review, 24*(4), 475–488.

Crenshaw, Kimberlé (1989). Demarginalizing the intersection of race and sex: A Black feminist critique of antidiscrimination doctrine, feminist theory and anti-racist politics. *University of Chicago Legal Forum, 1989*(1), 139–167.

Crenshaw, Kimberlé (1991). Mapping the margins: Intersectionality, identity politics, and violence against women of color. *Stanford Law Review, 43*(6), 1241–1299.

Crenshaw, Kimberlé (2020). 'Difference' through intersectionality 1. In S. Arya & A. S. Rathore (Eds.), *Dalit Feminist Theory: A Reader* (pp. 139–149): Routledge.

Diaz-Kope, Luisa M., Miller-Stevens, Katrina, & Henley, Tiffany J. (2019). An examination of dissertation research: The relationship between gender, methodological approach, and research design. *Journal of Public Affairs Education, 25*(1), 93–114.

Ding, Fangda, Lu, Jiahuan, & Riccucci, Norma M. (2021). How bureaucratic representation affects public organizational performance: A meta-analysis. *Public Administration Review, 81*(6), 1003–1018.

Dwiedienawati, Diena, Tjahjana, David, Faisal, M., Gandasari, Dyah, & Abdinagoro, Sri B. (2021). Determinants of perceived effectiveness in crisis management and company reputation during the COVID-19 pandemic. *Cogent Business & Management, 8*(1), 1912523.

Elias, Nicole M., & D'Agostino, Maria J. (2019). Gender competency in public administration education. *Teaching Public Administration, 37*(2), 218–233.

Evans, Michelle D., Irizarry, Jose L., & Freeman, J. Kenzie (2022). Disciplines, demographics, & expertise: Foundations for transferring professional norms in nonprofit graduate education. *Public Integrity*, 1–14.

Fink, Steven (1986). *Crisis management: Planning for the inevitable* (1st ed.). New York: AMACOM.

George, Elizabeth S., & Wesley, Mareena S. (2021). Marital stress and domestic violence during the COVID- 19 pandemic. *Cogent Arts & Humanities, 8*(1).

Henson, Cassandra R. (2019). Public value co-creation: A pedagogical approach to preparing future public administrators for collaboration. *Teaching Public Administration, 37*(3), 327–340.

Hough, Heather (2021). *COVID-19, the educational equity crisis, and the opportunity ahead.* Brown Center Chalkboard. Brookings Institute. Retrieved from www.brookings.edu/blog/brown-center-chalkboard/2021/04/29/covid-19-theeducational-equity-crisis-and-the-opportunity-ahead/

Hunt, Melissa G., Bogue, Kelsey, & Rohrbaugh, Nick (2012). Pet ownership and evacuation prior to Hurricane Irene. *Animals, 2*(4), 529–539.

Knepper, Hillary J., Sonenberg, Andrea, & Levine, Helisse (2018). The socio-environmental context of our actions: Marginalization and its influence on building a culture of health. *Journal of Health and Human Services Administration, 40*(4), 391–396.

Lebovits, Hannah, & Teal, Jennifer (2020). Considering equity in public process improvement trainings. *Public Integrity, 22*(6), 555–574.

Maji, Sucharita, Bansod, Saurabh, & Singh, Tushar (2022). Domestic violence during COVID-19 pandemic: The case for Indian women. *Journal of Community & Applied Social Psychology, 32*(3), 374–381.

Mitroff, Ian I., Shrivastava, Paul, & Udwadia, Firdaus E. (1987). Effective crisis management. *Academy of Management Perspectives, 1*(4), 283–292.

Monroe, Rev. Irene (2006, August 30). Katrina's legacy, one year later. *The Bay Area Reporter.* Retrieved from www.ebar.com/story.php?235639

Newberry, Michelle (2017). Pets in danger: Exploring the link between domestic violence and animal abuse. *Aggression and Violent Behavior, 34*, 273–281.

Nichols, Catherine (2015). Homme de Plume: What I learned sending my novel out under a male name. *Jezebel.* Retrieved from https://jezebel.com/homme-de-plume-what-ilearned-sending-my-novel-out-und-1720637627

Stukes, Patricia A. (2014). *A caravan of hope-gay Christian service: Exploring social vulnerability and capacity-building of lesbian, gay, bisexual, transgender and intersex identified individuals and organizational advocacy in two post Katrina disaster environments* (Ph.D.). ProQuest Dissertations Publishing.

Theobald, Hildegard (2017). Care workers with migration backgrounds in formal care services in Germany: A multi-level intersectional analysis. *International Journal of Care and Caring, 1*(2), 209–226.

Usher, Kim, Bhullar, Navjot, Durkin, Joanne, Gyamfi, Naomi, & Jackson, Debra (2020). Family violence and COVID-19: Increased vulnerability and reduced options for support. *International Journal of Mental Health Nursing, 29*(4), 549–552.

Whetstone, Crystal, & Demiroz, Fatih (2023). Understanding intersectionality and vulnerable populations: A missing part in building disaster resilient communities? In H. J. Knepper, M. D. Evans, & T. J. Henley (Eds.), *Intersectionality & crisis management: A path towards social equity.* New York: Routledge.

Appendix A
Chapter Discussion Questions and Prompts

Chapter 1

1. What is your understanding and interpretation of intersectionality?
2. Why should we explore crisis and intersectionality?
3. How can cultural competency improve social equity?
4. Provide examples of how cultural norms have affected your decision-making. In contrast, provide examples of how social norms and civic actions have affected organizational decision making.
5. Provide your own examples that need to be updated, given your understanding of intersectionality and crisis, similar to Table 1, which provides an opportunity to reconsider terminology.

Chapter 2

1) How can communities build social capital within the framework of intersectionality?
2) How has society contributed to further marginalizing people during crisis?
3) What are some strategies that can be employed to build resilient communities that focus on intersectionality and social equity?
4) What are some challenges faced by vulnerable populations seeking help during crisis?
5) How should administrators and managers factor in social, cultural, and religious beliefs in responding to crisis?

Chapter 3

1) How can intersectionality promote equitable policies and practices in healthcare?
2) How do cultural, political, economic, and societal factors affect local hospitals and health care organizations in your area?

3) How do social inequalities differ for healthcare professionals and patients during crisis?
4) How can administrators address burnout, especially for marginalized employees, during crisis?
5) What are some management strategies that employers can utilize to advance social equity in healthcare?

Chapter 4

1) How can HRM achieve effective performance outcomes while considering intersectionality, particularly during crisis?
2) Identify workplace equity challenges that can arise during times of crisis and offer recommendations.
3) Provide examples of how HRM can develop more equitable and inclusive policies.
4) Provide recommendations for how HRM policies could prevent women from falling through the cracks at the macro, meso, and micro levels.

Chapter 5

1) How do recent changes in statutory and case laws benefit or impact individuals based on privileged or marginalized populations?
2) How can intersectionality advance social equity through legal means?
3) How can nonprofit organizations balance competing forces such as funders with stipulations and governing boards while meeting the needs of vulnerable populations during times of crisis?
4) What kinds of strategies can public sector organizations utilize to address intersectional inequalities during crisis when delivering public services?

Chapter 6

1. How can intersectionality and crisis advance the ideals and principles of social equity?
2. How does the traditional model of crisis management differ from the integrative crisis management model? Why does it matter?
3. How can managers use an intersectional crisis management framework to improve business operations?
4. How can policymakers use an intersectional crisis management framework to improve policies?
5. How can academics use an intersectional crisis management framework to bridge the gap between theory and practice?

Appendix B
Glossary of Terms and Abbreviations

AAPI acronym for individuals who identify as Asian American and/or Pacific Islander.

Ableism term used to describe discrimination or exclusion in favor of able-bodied people. In this text we use (dis)ability to be inclusive of both able-bodied and those with physical, mental, or other cognitive challenges.

Ally term used to describe someone who is actively supportive of other classifications   i.e. LGBTQ+ ally.

ASPA American Society for Public Administration is an 83-year-old association of practitioners, academics, and students who work and study in the discipline of public administration and public service.

Binary Gender (also referred to as Sex) strict categories of male or female.

BIPOC used to describe a range of racial identities, acronym for Black, Indigenous, People of Color (see also People of Color).

Caste term refers to the social classification in Hindu societies, usually defined by heredity.

CDC Centers for Disease Control, sometimes referred to as Centers for Disease Control and Prevention.

Cisgender term used to describe a person whose gender identity aligns with the binary sex assigned at birth. Term highlights the privilege attached to those who are not transgender.

COMPA Conference of Minority Public Administrators.

Crisis significant, unexpected, urgent, or intense situations outside the normal or day-to-day environment. Can refer to natural, man-made, large scale (such as pandemic), or small scale (fire), see Chapter 1 for more discussion.

Culture (also organizational culture) values, beliefs, customs, or norms shared by a group (or people, employees, etc.) that influence assimilation of actions and behavior.

DEI   Diversity, equity, and inclusion.

Disability/(Dis)ability (see also ableism)   a social construct that identifies restrictions or lack of ability to perform activities considered "typical" for the average individual.

Discrimination   inequitable, unjust, or prejudicial treatment for categories of people (e.g. race, age, sex, etc.) by a dominant group or system against members of a marginalized group.

DSJ   acronym for the ASPA Section on Democracy and Social Justice.

Ethnicity   a social construct based on characteristics related to a national or cultural tradition.

FEMA   Federal Emergency Management Agency, oversees emergency personnel to prepare for, protect against, and respond to hazards and disasters.

Gender-fluid   individuals who do not identify with a single fixed gender or have fluid gender identities.

Gender identity   the gender that an individual uses to describe themselves. May or may not match the binary gender assigned at birth.

Gender non-conforming   individuals who do not conform with traditional expectations or expressions associated with a specific gender. Individuals *may or may not* also identify as transgender.

Genderqueer   individuals typically reject notions of rigid classifications of gender and embrace a fluidity of identity that may or may not always reflect sexual orientation. Individuals may or may not view themselves as both male and female or be classified outside of binary categories.

Hegemony/Hegemonic   term used to describe a dominance or authority over others, often related to traditional social, cultural, or economic influences.

HR or HRM   Human resource/s (HR) or Human resource/s management.

IBPA Framework   acronym for Intersectionality-Based Policy Analysis.

Intersectionality   a term coined to describe the overlapping and interconnected attributes, such as race, gender, and socioeconomic status, that serve to increase marginalization and burdens in society. This term is frequently associated with scholar Kimberlé Crenshaw.

LatinX   term used generally in the academic community to describe the range of race/ethnicities that include Hispanic, Latino/Latina, Caucasian/Hispanic origin. Term is intended to be inclusive and gender-neutral.

LGBTQ+   sometimes referred to as LGBT or LGBTQIA. Acronym for lesbian, gay, bisexual, transgender, queer/questioning.

Neurodivergent   having a brain that functions in ways that diverge significantly from the dominant societal standards of "normal." Commonly associated in reference to autistic spectrum disorders.

"New Normal"   term used to describe changing workplace trends as a result of COVID-19. Trends include work from home, hybrid work, remote work, telecommuting, technology, and changing expectations.

NGO   acronym stands for non-government organization that functions independently of government. NGO is often used for nonprofits based outside of the US.

Patriarchy/Patriarchal   relating to a system of society or government historically dominated by men.

People of color/Person of color   term used to describe the range of race/ethnicities that are considered non-white. Includes, but not limited to, Black, Asian, LatinX, Native American/Indigenous. See also BIPOC. Other variations include Women of color.

PPE   Personal protective equipment.

Praxis   term used to describe the practical application of theory.

Public sector   broad term used to describe issues, policies, and responsibility connected to both the government and nonprofit sector.

Race   social construct based on characteristics such as appearance or physical characteristics, especially skin color. Often paired with ethnicity given the overlap of racial characteristics with national or cultural heritage.

Sexual orientation   based upon romantic or sexual attraction to other people. Sexual orientation is different and independent of gender identity.

"She-cession"   new term to describe the disproportionate number of women who left, or were forced to leave, the paid workforce during or as a result of changing dynamics during COVID-19, and/or the financial impacts related to changing COVID-19 dynamics.

Social capital   term used to define the value of relationships among people, individually, and in groups, it can include networks and may contain expectations of reciprocity.

Sociocultural   term used to describe the combination of social and cultural factors, including habits, traditions, beliefs, religion, demographics, and social classes.

Social equity   term used to describe the pursuit of fairness, particularly in public service, in regard to access, outcomes, quality, and process through addressing systemic inequities faced by marginalized communities.

Socioeconomic   term used to describe income, education level, occupation, and social status of individuals and groups.

STEMM   acronym for Science, Technology, Engineering, Math, and Medicine.

Telecommuting or hybrid work the practice of working fully or partially from home, often through the use of technology such as video/teleconference, etc.

Transgender term used to describe an individual whose gender identity does not match and/or and conform to societal/cultural expectations based on the binary sex assigned at birth.

Transitioning a process that some transgender people undergo to live their lives more fully as their "true gender." Generally includes additional steps such as social transition, changing name/pronouns, hormone treatment, or gender affirming surgery.

UN United Nations

USAID U.S. Agency for International Development

NOTE: A more detailed listing of gender and sexual orientation terms can be found at the HRC and LGBTQIA websites below.

List includes some terms pulled from the following websites

Human Rights Campaign [HRC]. (n.d.). *Glossary of terms*. Retrieved from www.hrc.org/resources/glossary-of-terms

LGBTQIA Resource Center. (2022). *LGBTIA resource center glossary*. Retrieved from https://lgbtqia.ucdavis.edu/educated/glossary

U.S. Census Bureau. (2022). *About the topic of race*. Retrieved from www.census.gov/topics/population/race/about.html

Index

Note: Numbers in **bold** indicate a table. Numbers in *italics* indicate a figure

Printed in the United States
by Baker & Taylor Publisher Services